The Son of God

THE SON OF GOD

Readings from the Gospel According to St. Mark

With Background Information by
Edric A. Weld
and
William Sydnor

Illustrated by Leonard Weisgard

Materials for Christian Education
Prepared at the Direction of General Convention

THE SEABURY PRESS
Greenwich, Connecticut

© 1957 by The Seabury Press, Incorporated

THE SEABURY SERIES is prepared for Christian education in parishes and missions by the National Council of the Protestant Episcopal Church in the United States of America at the direction of the General Convention.

>THE REV. DAVID R. HUNTER, ED.D.
>   Director
>   Department of Christian Education
>
>THE REV. LESTER W. MCMANIS, M.A.
>   Executive Secretary
>   Division of Curriculum Development

Library of Congress Catalogue Card Number:
57-8343

Scripture quotations in *The Son of God* are from *The Revised Standard Version of the Bible,* copyrighted 1946 and 1952 by the Division of Christian Education, National Council of Churches.

240-760-HK-50-25
SECOND PRINTING, 1960
PRINTED IN THE UNITED STATES OF AMERICA

Contents

	About This Book	1
Chapter 1	The Way It Started	3
	St. Mark 1:1–13	
Chapter 2	Follow Me	12
	St. Mark 1:14–39; 2:1–28; 3:1–6	
Chapter 3	Popularity	30
	St. Mark 3:7–35; 4:1–9, 26–41; 5:1–43; 6:1–16	
Chapter 4	Feeding the Five Thousand	44
	St. Mark 6:30–52; 7:24–37	
Chapter 5	Who Is He?	52
	St. Mark 8:27–38; 9:2–41	
Chapter 6	The Challenge	62
	St. Mark 10:1–52; 11:1–11	

Chapter 7	Jesus Meets His Enemies		78
	St. Mark 11:15–19, 27–33; 12:1–44; 13:1–2; 14:1–31		
Chapter 8	Trials		96
	St. Mark 14:32–50, 53–72; 15:1–15		
Chapter 9	The Way of the Cross		110
	St. Mark 15:16–39		
Chapter 10	The First Easter		116
	St. Mark 15:42–47; 16:1–8		

About This Book

THIS book is intended to help you read the Gospel According to St. Mark. The plan is to provide you with background information which will make it possible for you to read St. Mark with understanding. Our hope is that this book will help you decide for yourself who Jesus of Nazareth is.

We have followed the account of Jesus' life as St. Mark gives it to us. This means that there are many familiar Gospel passages which you will miss. For example, the Christmas stories, the Beatitudes, the parables of the Good Samaritan and the Prodigal Son, the Ascension, are not mentioned in St. Mark's account, and so they are not included. This does not mean we consider them unimportant. It only means that this book gives you the portrait of Jesus which St. Mark painted for his readers, Romans who had just become Christians.

It is probable that you have many questions about Jesus Christ which have not been answered. Perhaps you can find the answers in this book. Also, if your family reads the Bible together, *The Son of God* will be a good book to use.

THE BEGINNING of the gospel of Jesus Christ, the Son of God.

Chapter 1

The Way It Started

WORD had spread that a prophet was preaching and baptizing in the Jordan River. Excited people were traveling over the roads and trails into the hot little valley far below sea level. Over brown hills and past dead rocks, they came from Jerusalem and other towns in the rocky hill-lands of Judea, or from the more gentle hills of Galilee.

There was excitement in the air, for the Jews believed that God acted directly in daily events. They knew their religious history, and they expected that God would send them a prophet. Perhaps this John the baptizer who was preaching on the banks of the Jordan was the prophet promised in their Bible (what we call the Old Testament) Perhaps, now, they could look forward to being an independent nation again.

There had been a time when the Jewish nation was free. But for the past century the Romans had ruled the Jews, taxed them, and governed them through a family of kings who were like puppets on a Roman string. They were called the Herods. There was also a Roman governor in Judea who collected, or procured, the taxes and kept the peace; he was called a *procurator*. The Jews naturally hated their Roman rulers and those who cooperated with them. They believed that God would send a Messiah to lead the Jews against the Romans. "Will this preacher, John, start a revolution?" they asked.

This was not the first time Israel had lost her independence. Ever since their escape from Egypt under Moses, the people had had to fight for their freedom. The Assyrians, the Babylonians, the Persians, the Egyptians, and others had controlled them; now it was the hated Romans.

There were several views among religious leaders as to why Israel had lost its independence. One view was that in the past, whenever the nation had sinned, God permitted foreigners to take over: the people had not obeyed God's laws, and that was now the trouble, they thought. This view grew out of the teaching of the rabbis in the synagogues, and the children learned it because the rabbis were their schoolteachers.

If the problem was as simple as this, there should have been an answer. But there was no agreement. Some of the rabbis who taught in the Temple in Jerusalem said that if only all the people of Israel would keep the Law of Moses perfectly for one day, God would deliver His people from the foreigners. However, there were always some people who broke the laws no matter how hard they tried. And there were always others who wouldn't even try to keep the laws. No day of perfect obedience was in sight, and therefore the situation looked hopeless.

Another view was held by those called Zealots, who were sure that if the people showed enough courage and zeal, freedom could be won. They remembered how David had killed Goliath and won the battle with the Philistines. Judas the Hammerer and his ragged army had driven out the armies of King Antiochus of Syria. If the people could show this same kind of courage again, they thought, God would send His appointed Saviour to lead them against the enemy, and victory would be certain.

The third view was held by the more thoughtful, who reasoned this way: "Judas and his Maccabee brothers beat the Syrians two hundred years ago, but before we could drive out the Romans, half of our men would be killed. God doesn't work that way any more. When God sends his Saviour, the Messiah, on the clouds of heaven, the world as we know it will end. Our enemies and all who hate us will be wiped out. The mighty will be put down, and the true Israel will live in righteousness and peace."

So there were three views: let's keep the Law perfectly; let's fight with all our might; let's have faith that God will send a divine Helper.

This was the situation when word spread among the people that a prophet was preaching, "The judgment day of God is at hand." Because the people expected God to do *something,* John's preaching excited them. They began to wonder who he was. He certainly dressed as a prophet, wearing coarse camel's-hair clothes held at the waist with a strip of leather. He reminded many who knew their Bible of an ancient prophet named Elijah who had turned Israel from the worship of idols. Some of these people thought that Elijah would return to earth before the day of judgment. They began to wonder if John were Elijah come to earth again. That could be a sign of the coming Day of the Lord! Maybe the Messiah was coming! This was exciting news for those who hoped that the Messiah would free Israel from the control of the Romans.

But John was doing more than preaching. He was baptizing his fellow Jews. After a foreigner had become a Jew, he was baptized as an extra rite to cleanse him from his previous idol worship. But John was preaching that *all* his listeners should be baptized, and they were flocking to him in great crowds! For the first time in many years a prophet had appeared, and he was preaching a "baptism of repentance." Those who wanted to be baptized had to confess their sins. God would forgive them, and they would be ready for the coming of the Messiah.

So the people came, all kinds of people, including the down-and-outers and the respectable ones. They confessed their sins, and they promised to change their way of life.

The people placed themselves in the water of the Jordan

River and said prayers asking for forgiveness of their sins. This was an act of preparation, for John said that after him would come the Messiah, who would baptize them with the Holy Spirit! This meant to his hearers that the spiritual presence of God would work in and through them, and they would have the power to be righteous. Therefore, they would be ready for God's act of becoming the king of all the people. There would be a kingdom of God on earth!

Is it any wonder that the first people who heard John preaching this astonishing message hurried home to tell their neighbors the news? "God has sent His Messenger! Salvation is at hand! Israel will be restored! Hurry and be baptized before it is too late!"

The Baptism of Jesus: *St. Mark 1:1–13*

1 The beginning of the gospel of Jesus Christ, the Son of God.
² As it is written in Isaiah the prophet,
"Behold, I send my messenger before thy face,
who shall prepare thy way;
³ the voice of one crying in the wilderness:
Prepare the way of the Lord,
make his paths straight—"
⁴ John the baptizer appeared in the wilderness, preaching a baptism of repentance for the forgiveness of sins.
⁵ And there went out to him all the country of Judea, and

all the people of Jerusalem; and they were baptized by him in the river Jordan, confessing their sins.

⁶ Now John was clothed with camel's hair, and had a leather girdle around his waist, and ate locusts and wild honey. ⁷And he preached, saying, "After me comes he who is mightier than I, the thong of whose sandals I am not worthy to stoop down and untie. ⁸I have baptized you with water; but he will baptize you with the Holy Spirit."

⁹ In those days Jesus came from Nazareth of Galilee and was baptized by John in the Jordan. ¹⁰And when he came up out of the water, immediately he saw the heavens opened and the Spirit descending upon him like a dove; ¹¹ and a voice came from heaven, "Thou art my beloved Son; with thee I am well pleased."

¹² The Spirit immediately drove him out into the wilderness. ¹³And he was in the wilderness forty days, tempted by Satan; and he was with the wild beasts; and the angels ministered to him.

The Decision

How do we know about the wonderful thing that happened to Jesus when John baptized him? At that time, Jesus had no disciples who might have witnessed what took place. St. Mark gives the impression that only Jesus knew what had occurred. Only he saw the heavens open and the Spirit descending and heard the voice.

Here is picture language describing a deeply spiritual

experience: "the Spirit descending upon him like a dove." Here is picture language telling us what Jesus heard: "Thou art my beloved Son; with thee I am well pleased." Something happened to Jesus at his baptism that was of supreme importance to the history of the world.

Jesus came away from his baptism in the Jordan River convinced that he was to be the chosen Deliverer long-promised by God to His people. Jesus now knew who he was, but no one else shared his secret. The rest of the Gospel is the story of what it meant to have God's own Son living on earth, and of how men came to learn who Jesus is.

Often people go away to be by themselves after learning what their job is going to be. This is what Jesus now did. What kind of Messiah was he going to be? He knew the Scriptures well. The words, "Thou art my beloved Son," which came to him were from the Psalms and referred to God's Messiah or Deliverer. But the Scriptures described the Messiah in several ways.

One popular idea was that God would send His Messiah as a military leader. He would be a strong king, like David, who would lead the Israelites in a revolution against the Romans. This hope that Israel could again be a nation standing on its own feet was a very strong one. Another view was that the Messiah would come in the manner of a heavenly being, on the clouds, and he would enter the life of the people and perform great miracles. Hidden in the Old Testament, and not so popular a view, was a picture of the servant of God who would take on himself the suffering of his people; through this suffering they would be forgiven their sins and made pure.

Jesus spent forty days and nights in the desert thinking through what it meant to be God's beloved Son. He battled with temptations to misuse his power, to take short-cuts in trying to help his people, and to be the wrong kind of Messiah. He prayed for the help he needed to make the right decision.

Then he left the wilderness and began his work.

Chapter 2

Follow Me

JOHN the baptizer had been preaching near the spot where the Jordan River empties into the Dead Sea. He was a big, rough-looking fellow with a voice to match. Standing on a rock, the hot desert breeze blowing through his hair and beard, he spoke to the crowds fearlessly and without hesitation. He told them that they must prepare themselves for the coming of God's Promised One, and he made it clear that everyone, no matter what his position or rank, was in need of repentance.

Shaking a bony finger in warning, he might cry: "Don't think it will do you any good to claim that you and your family have always kept the Sabbath. Live out your faith in daily life, else how are you better than the stones in the wall which also hear the rabbis teach?"

Or another time, "You tax collectors," he might call to those unpopular men, "be strictly honest and fair."

Even the Roman soldiers who were on hand to keep the peace came under his eagle eye. "See that you don't rob the people, and do not bully them," he cried.

Finally, someone said to John, "What about King Herod? What should he do?" And John answered boldly, without a pause, "Herod must stop living with his brother's wife and repent!"

A gasp went up from the tense crowd, for it was dangerous to criticize the authorities, especially King Herod who had listeners everywhere to spot and report troublemakers. Shortly after, John was arrested. He was imprisoned in a grim fortress where there was little chance of escape.

Just about this time, some seventy miles north of the Dead Sea on the shore of the Sea of Galilee near Capernaum, Jesus began to preach.

The Jordan River wanders back and forth like a snake track as it drops from the Sea of Galilee to the Dead Sea almost 1300 feet below sea level. Along its banks are green valleys, but, nearby, steep hills shoot up toward the sky. The hilly country is sunbaked and brown, and the roads are dusty.

In those days, Capernaum was a trading and fishing center on the main road between Egypt and the east. Along this road came large caravans of travelers, merchants, and pilgrims. Some of the people walked; others rode or put their wares on the backs of camels and donkeys. The people traveled together for safety against the bands of robbers who attacked individuals or small groups. There was a military post of Roman soldiers stationed in Capernaum to protect the travelers, and there was also a Roman toll station where the tolls used to support the road were collected. Because there were always soldiers in the narrow streets, the people were constantly reminded that they were under the hated Roman rule.

The district in which Capernaum was located was called Galilee. In this area were many Jews and many, called proselytes, who had previously been Gentiles but who had joined the Jewish faith. There were also those who worshiped Zeus and other Greek gods. The capital city of Tiberias, eight miles south of Capernaum, was mostly Greek, and the strictest Jews would not enter the city. King Herod, who was not a full-blooded Jew, lived in Tiberias like a Greek and found life in the capital city very pleasant.

It was not surprising that the people of Judea to the south, and especially those who lived in old Jerusalem, looked down on the Galileans as being not very strict Jews in their religious practices. Yet Galilee was the region in which interest in the coming of God's Deliverer was the strongest. Most of the fiery Zealots who were eager to take the sword and drive out the Roman invaders also lived in Galilee.

It was the usual thing in those days for a teacher, or rabbi, to sit out of doors while he talked to his followers. If he went for a walk, a group of listeners would usually go with him. From these followers he often selected a special group of disciples, to whom he gave additional instruction.

The call to be a disciple of a rabbi was serious business. When a rabbi said to a young man, "Follow me," what he meant was, "Leave your family and your business and your home and your possessions and become one of my special pupils." If a man accepted this invitation, he left all his former life behind and lived wherever his rabbi lived. He followed his rabbi obediently and saw that all the rabbi's needs were met. A disciple had to do all the things a personal slave would do except to stoop down and untie his master's sandals. (When John the baptizer said that he was not worthy even to untie the sandals of the Coming One, he meant that Christ would be so much greater than he that he would not be worthy even to be his slave.)

Most important, a disciple was expected to memorize everything his rabbi taught him. This is the way learning was passed on. The rabbi spoke for a certain length of time, and then he stopped and listened to his disciples who were expected to repeat what he had said. If they made a mistake, they tried again. In this way, they finally memorized all of the teaching of their rabbi. The other part of the disciples' responsibility was perhaps even more important, for by living with their teacher they learned from his example. Thus the rabbi and his disciples made a very special kind of group. A disciple remained with his rabbi until he had learned all that his rabbi could teach him. Then he became a rabbi himself.

The family unit was very important to Jews. A man

stayed in his father's household, with his wife and children, until his father died. Nothing was allowed to break the family circle except one special thing: the call to become a disciple of a rabbi.

Jesus had grown up in Nazareth, a town near the center of the district of Galilee. It is therefore not surprising that he began his work in Galilee and that his first disciples were Galileans.

After telling how Jesus called his first disciples, St. Mark describes the things which happened on a typical day in Capernaum. This particular day was the Sabbath. The custom was for the man in charge of the synagogue service to ask a visiting rabbi to preach. When Jesus was invited to teach, the people were astonished.

A Typical Sabbath: *St. Mark 1:14–39*

1 Now after John was arrested, Jesus came into Galilee, preaching the gospel of God, [15]and saying, "The time is fulfilled, and the kingdom of God is at hand; repent, and believe in the gospel."

[16]And passing along by the Sea of Galilee, he saw Simon and Andrew the brother of Simon casting a net in the sea; for they were fishermen. [17]And Jesus said to them, "Follow me and I will make you become fishers of men." [18]And immediately they left their nets and followed him. [19]And going on a little farther, he saw James the son of Zebedee and John his brother, who were in their boat mending the

nets. ²⁰And immediately he called them; and they left their father Zebedee in the boat with the hired servants, and followed him.

²¹And they went into Capernaum; and immediately on the sabbath he entered the synagogue and taught. ²²And they were astonished at his teaching, for he taught them as one who had authority, and not as the scribes.

²³And immediately there was in their synagogue a man with an unclean spirit; ²⁴ and he cried out, "What have you to do with us, Jesus of Nazareth? Have you come to destroy us? I know who you are, the Holy One of God."

²⁵ But Jesus rebuked him, saying, "Be silent, and come out of him!" ²⁶And the unclean spirit, convulsing him and crying with a loud voice, came out of him.

²⁷And they were all amazed, so that they questioned among themselves, saying, "What is this? A new teaching! With authority he commands even the unclean spirits, and they obey him." ²⁸And at once his fame spread everywhere throughout all the surrounding region of Galilee.

²⁹And immediately he left the synagogue, and entered the house of Simon and Andrew, with James and John. ³⁰ Now Simon's mother-in-law lay sick with a fever, and immediately they told him of her. ³¹And he came and took her by the hand and lifted her up, and the fever left her; and she served them.

³² That evening, at sundown, they brought to him all who were sick or possessed with demons. ³³And the whole city was gathered together about the door. ³⁴And he healed many who were sick with various diseases, and cast out

many demons; and he would not permit the demons to speak, because they knew him.

³⁵And in the morning, a great while before day, he rose and went out to a lonely place, and there he prayed. ³⁶And Simon and those who were with him followed him, ³⁷ and they found him and said to him, "Every one is searching for you." ³⁸And he said to them, "Let us go on to the next towns, that I may preach there also; for that is why I came out." ³⁹And he went throughout all Galilee, preaching in their synagogues and casting out demons.

Why They Marveled

IT TOOK courage for those first four disciples to sell their fishing boats and give up their homes and their jobs in order to follow Jesus of Nazareth. No doubt they were drawn to him in part by the warmth of his spirit and the way in which his presence and words made God seem close at hand. Almost as soon as they became Jesus' followers, three other things about him must have caused these fishermen to marvel, and also must have made them excited.

First, there was a "can't wait" atmosphere about this rabbi from Nazareth. It was as though he were carrying out orders so important that they had to be done at once. The disciples saw that it was very important to him to tell everyone about the kingdom of God. He did this in Capernaum, and then, in spite of his popularity, he insisted on leaving. He acted like a soldier under orders.

The second thing they must have found exciting about Jesus was that evil spirits obeyed him. These unclean spirits, or demons, were the forces of evil that made people bad or sick or crazy. When God's kingdom had fully come, demons would no longer have power to drive people crazy or tear them apart, the Jews believed. Because Jesus had the power to heal people, it was a sign that God's kingdom had begun to come in him. People were amazed that Jesus had this power.

The third thing about Jesus which caused them to be excited was the way in which he taught. Not only the disciples but also others who heard him realized that he knew what he was doing. He did not need to quote Scripture: he simply spoke the truth, and it stood on its own authority.

But even though the people recognized Jesus' authority, they did not understand how he was able to command it; and neither did the disciples. They could only marvel at such a person.

The unclean spirits seemed to know who Jesus was, but no one paid attention to them.

The Crowd

WHAT were the people like who heard Jesus speak? Of his many kinds of listeners, the most impressive were the Pharisees. Among the religious-minded Jews, the

Pharisees were, so to speak, the nobility. They were the party or brotherhood who treasured and studied and kept the Law of Moses. This Law, the Torah as it was called, was found in the first five books of the Bible. It was God's will for all the people, the Jews believed. The Pharisees were the religious leaders of the people, but they were not priests. They made it their business to explain and interpret the many laws so that men could understand and keep them.

Some of the most important laws were not always clear, and they needed to be explained. For example, the Fourth Commandment forbids "work" on the Sabbath, but the people were not certain in their minds what was work and what was not. So some careful definitions were given: it was work to walk two miles, to sew two stitches, to lift two dried figs, to write two letters of a word, or even to erase two letters!

Eventually, in answering the question, "What *work* is forbidden on the Sabbath?" the Pharisees drew up a list of thirty-nine rules. This was called "building a fence around the Law," to make sure that no one broke it by mistake. Of course, it was work to carry a sick person, and it would certainly be work to heal anyone.

The Pharisees were greatly respected. They loved God's Law. They understood the Law. They kept the Law.

Within the party of the Pharisees was a very special group known as scribes. Books in those days were handwritten on scrolls of parchment and had to be copied. The scribes were the copyists who produced additional scrolls. When you have to copy something many times, you learn it pretty well. The scribes, therefore, became the experts on the Law and were like lawyers.

When a Pharisee or any other Jew wanted a copy of Deuteronomy or Exodus, for example, he asked a scribe to make the copy for him. If he did not understand how the Law was to be applied, a scribe could tell him what his duty was. The scribes told the people with whom they could associate. There were many Greeks in Galilee, and a strict Jew would be considered legally unclean if he associated with them or any other Gentiles. After such contact, he could not take part in Jewish festivals until he had purified himself. To avoid this danger, the Pharisees drew up another set of rules including one which forbade eating with non-Jews. Some rabbis carried this even further: "You must not eat with anyone who eats with Gentiles."

Many of the people who wanted to serve God were confused by all of these rules. They could not remember them, and keeping all of them was impossible. So many people began to think that God was a hard taskmaster.

Others gave up trying to keep the rules. The Pharisees called these people "sinners." Among these "sinners" were those who had to work from dawn until dark or who had to farm a small patch of ground. They had no time to study either the 613 written laws in the Torah or the many rules drawn up by the rabbis to help people keep the laws. They could not possibly keep all the regulations on what clothes to wear, how to wash, how to prepare food, what kind of cooking dishes to use, and all the rest.

The Pharisees had come to believe that God loved people to the extent to which they kept the Law. They meant the Law as defined by all the rules and regulations. They could not see how God would waste His love on the common people. So the common people gave up worrying very much about the Law or about God. But they needed help from God to keep them strong in soul, and this, they felt, was denied to them.

It was bad enough for healthy people to feel shut out from God, but it was even worse for sick people. In those days, everyone believed that sickness was a sign that God had not yet forgiven a sinner. The Pharisees believed that God required some proof of repentance before He would forgive. It was almost as if a person had to do enough good things to balance the bad before he could be forgiven.

These, then, were the kinds of people in the crowds who heard Jesus preach and who witnessed his healing love: (1) the strict Pharisees and scribes who knew and kept the Law; (2) discouraged common people who longed for God's love; (3) pitiable sick ones from whom other men kept away lest they catch God's disapproval; (4) "sinners" who had given up trying to be faithful to God's Law; and (5) an occasional madman, possessed of evil spirits, shunned, laughed at, and feared.

The First Conflicts: *St. Mark 2:1–28; 3:1–6*

2 And when he returned to Capernaum after some days, it was reported that he was at home. ² And many were gathered together, so that there was no longer room for them, not even about the door; and he was preaching the

word to them. ³ And they came, bringing to him a paralytic carried by four men. ⁴ And when they could not get near him because of the crowd, they removed the roof above him; and when they had made an opening, they let down the pallet on which the paralytic lay. ⁵ And when Jesus saw their faith, he said to the paralytic, "My son, your sins are forgiven."

⁶ Now some of the scribes were sitting there, questioning in their hearts. ⁷ "Why does this man speak thus? It is blasphemy! Who can forgive sins but God alone?"

⁸ And immediately Jesus, perceiving in his spirit that they thus questioned within themselves, said to them, "Why do you question thus in your hearts? ⁹ Which is easier, to say to the paralytic, 'Your sins are forgiven,' or to say, 'Rise, take up your pallet and walk'? ¹⁰ But that you may know that the Son of man has authority on earth to forgive sins"—he said to the paralytic—¹¹ "I say to you, rise, take up your pallet and go home."

¹² And he rose, and immediately took up the pallet and went out before them all; so that they were all amazed and glorified God, saying, "We never saw anything like this!"

¹³ He went out again beside the sea; and all the crowd gathered about him, and he taught them. ¹⁴ And as he passed on, he saw Levi the son of Alphaeus sitting at the tax office, and he said to him, "Follow me." And he rose and followed him.

¹⁵ And as he sat at table in his house, many tax collectors and sinners were sitting with Jesus and his disciples; for there were many who followed him. ¹⁶ And the scribes of

the Pharisees, when they saw that he was eating with sinners and tax collectors, said to his disciples, "Why does he eat with tax collectors and sinners?"

¹⁷ And when Jesus heard it, he said to them, "Those who are well have no need of a physician, but those who are sick; I came not to call the righteous, but sinners."

¹⁸ Now John's disciples and the Pharisees were fasting; and people came and said to him, "Why do John's disciples and the disciples of the Pharisees fast, but your disciples do not fast?"

¹⁹ And Jesus said to them, "Can the wedding guests fast while the bridegroom is with them? As long as they have the bridegroom with them, they cannot fast. ²⁰ The days will come, when the bridegroom is taken away from them, and then they will fast in that day. ²¹ No one sews a piece of unshrunk cloth on an old garment; if he does, the patch tears away from it, the new from the old, and a worse tear is made. ²² And no one puts new wine into old wineskins; if he does, the wine will burst the skins, and the wine is lost, and so are the skins; but new wine is for fresh skins."

²³ One sabbath he was going through the grainfields; and as they made their way his disciples began to pluck ears of grain. ²⁴ And the Pharisees said to him, "Look, why are they doing what is not lawful on the sabbath?"

²⁵ And he said to them, "Have you never read what David did, when he was in need and was hungry, he and those who were with him. ²⁶ how he entered the house of God, when Abiathar was high priest, and ate the bread of the Presence, which it is not lawful for any but the priests

to eat, and also gave it to those who were with him?" [27] And he said to them, "The sabbath was made for man, not man for the sabbath; [28] so the Son of man is lord even of the sabbath."

3 Again he entered the synagogue, and a man was there who had a withered hand. [2] And they watched him, to see whether he would heal him on the sabbath, so that they might accuse him. [3] And he said to the man who had the withered hand, "Come here." [4] And he said to them, "Is it lawful on the sabbath to do good or to do harm, to save life or to kill?" But they were silent. [5] And he looked around at them with anger, grieved at their hardness of heart, and said to the man, "Stretch out your hand." He stretched it out, and his hand was restored. [6] The Pharisees went out, and immediately held counsel with the Herodians against him, how to destroy him.

The First Enemies

WOULDN'T you think that people as devout as the Pharisees would have welcomed Jesus? Here was a new rabbi who was attracting great crowds. People who had lost hope were now seriously thinking of God's Word. Shouldn't this have made the Pharisees happy? Why didn't they support and encourage Jesus?

To many of the Pharisees, Jesus was dangerous. If Jesus had his way, they thought, the duty of keeping the Law would be ignored. The whole religious outlook would be changed. Look what Jesus was doing!

First, in the synagogue Jesus *offered* forgiveness to the paralyzed man before the fellow had earned it. Such a thing was blasphemy, for it belittled God's way of forgiving. God's forgiveness was not freely given to anyone who might want it. One had to work for it. Anyone who misled people in this way was dangerous. Such a person should be stopped.

Second, Jesus associated with the wrong people. No righteous man would mix with "sinners," at least until they changed their ways. Jesus even included tax collectors in his company. These Jews who collected the Roman taxes were classed with "sinners" for two reasons: (1) they were often dishonest grafters who charged people more than they owed; (2) because of their dealings with Gentiles they were "unclean." No righteous man would associate with tax collectors, but Jesus did. Of course, the Pharisees wanted sinners to repent. But until they did the Pharisees would have nothing to do with them. The high standards of the Law must be upheld. So Jesus was setting a very bad example. He was dangerous. He must be stopped.

Third, Jesus did not pay enough attention to the ancient, honored customs of the Jewish religion. These "traditions of the elders," as they were called, laid great stress on prayer, fasting, and almsgiving. The more one observed these three honored customs, and the more openly, the more pious one was thought to be. Some Pharisees went so far as to say prayers aloud on street corners. Almsgiving and fasting were also done in such a way that people could not help but see. Men fasted to show their sorrow for their sins. They also fasted to show their sorrow for the sins of the nation, especially for those sins which kept God's Deliverer from coming to save his people.

Jesus had a reputation for not fasting, although of course he had fasted at the time of his temptation in the wilderness. When the Pharisees questioned him about why he and his disciples did not fast, Jesus' answer shocked them. He said that the news of the dawn of God's kingdom made every day as joyful as a wedding day. Sorrow and fasting were out of the question at such a time. New traditions were being made which did not fit the traditions of the elders, any more than new wine could be held in old leather bags which would no longer stretch. This Jesus was a dangerous kind of teacher. He was undermining the ancient, honored customs of the Jewish religion.

For many of the Pharisees, keeping the Sabbath was the most important law of all. In order to keep the Sabbath day holy, they carefully avoided any suggestion of work which might break that law. They were angered at Jesus when he and his disciples, as they walked through a grain field on the Sabbath, rubbed the outer husk from kernels of grain between the palms of their hands and ate the grain.

"Work," said the Pharisees. "Threshing grain is work, no matter how small the amount."

The Pharisees became further shocked when, in answer to their criticism, Jesus explained the use of the Sabbath in a new way. "The Sabbath was made for man," he said. God provided a day of rest and worship for the benefit of man. Here Jesus was going behind the actual words of the Law to explain what God intended by the Law. But the Pharisees rejected his explanation. Jesus was, in their eyes, destroying the Law.

Now Jesus had some real enemies. The Pharisees, good and respectable as they were, saw Jesus as one who was pulling to pieces the precious practices and laws and customs which the Jews had accepted for hundreds of years. They began to plot how they might destroy him.

Chapter 3

Popularity

ONE OF the first questions asked about a teacher whose teaching causes astonishment is, "How is he being received? What do people think of him? Are they coming out to hear him? Is his popularity going to last?"

During the first weeks of Jesus' ministry, the people who heard him and witnessed his healing of sick people were tremendously excited. Many liked him and were impressed, astonished, and overjoyed by what he said and did. Some were not so sure about him. Still others, the Pharisees especially, thought he was dangerous. Some of those who wanted to be freed from Roman rule through revolution hoped he might become the leader of the armies. The

Pharisees feared that Jesus' popularity might lead to rebellion, and they began to plot with King Herod's friends how they might destroy Jesus.

If you had lived in Capernaum over nineteen hundred years ago, you probably would have gone out to hear Jesus. But how far would you have traveled to hear a new rabbi whose teaching was said to be good news to people in distress? Ten miles? Twenty? There were no buses, and you would have had to walk or ride a donkey.

Or perhaps you would have believed the reports that he was really healing the sick. Would you have carried your ailing friend or mother fifty miles hoping that the reports were true? Remember that there were no trains, no automobiles, no paved highways. You would have had to walk, and even your sandals would not have provided much protection for your feet on the sandy, gravelly, bumpy roads.

There were no newspapers, no radio or television, and yet the news of this new rabbi from Nazareth spread over most of Palestine. Jerusalem was eighty miles south, yet the people there had heard of him. The region of Idumea was thirty miles beyond Jerusalem through the mountains, but the people there, too, had heard of Jesus. The distance from Tyre to Capernaum was not great, but to go from one city to the other, travelers had to cross a mountain pass 4000 feet high. Sidon was almost as far away as Damascus. Yet people came in great numbers from Idumea and Tyre and Sidon, and news of Jesus traveled wherever men gathered throughout the land.

But popularity had its problems. First, Jesus needed additional helpers. The four disciples he had already chosen could not begin to do the job. Then, as is frequently true, there were those who were jealous of this winsome, popular leader, and they began to say mean things about him. A third problem was Jesus' own family, who did not understand why he had left home and who wanted him to stop this preaching and return to the carpenter shop.

The Kingdom of God
St. Mark 3:7–35; 4:1–9, 26–34

3 Jesus withdrew with his disciples to the sea, and a great multitude from Galilee followed; also from Judea [8] and Jerusalem and Idumea and from beyond the Jordan and from about Tyre and Sidon a great multitude, hearing all that he did, came to him. [9] And he told his disciples to have a boat ready for him because of the crowd, lest they should crush him; [10] for he had healed many, so that all who had diseases pressed upon him to touch him. [11] And whenever the unclean spirits beheld him, they fell down before him and cried out, "You are the Son of God." [12] And he strictly ordered them not to make him known.

[13] And he went up into the hills, and called to him those whom he desired; and they came to him. [14] And he appointed twelve, to be with him, and to be sent out to preach [15] and have authority to cast out demons: [16] Simon whom he surnamed Peter; [17] James the son of Zebedee and

John the brother of James, whom he surnamed Boanerges, that is, sons of thunder; ¹⁸ Andrew, and Philip, and Bartholomew, and Matthew, and Thomas, and James the son of Alphaeus, and Thaddaeus, and Simon the Cananaean, ¹⁹ and Judas Iscariot, who betrayed him.

Then he went home; ²⁰ and the crowd came together again, so that they could not even eat. ²¹ And when his friends heard it, they went out to seize him, for they said, "He is beside himself."

²² And the scribes who came down from Jerusalem said, "He is possessed by Beelzebul, and by the prince of demons he casts out the demons." ²³ And he called them to him, and said to them in parables, "How can Satan cast out Satan? ²⁴ If a kingdom is divided against itself, that kingdom cannot stand. ²⁵ And if a house is divided against itself, that house will not be able to stand. ²⁶ And if Satan has risen up against himself and is divided, he cannot stand, but is coming to an end. ²⁷ But no one can enter a strong man's house and plunder his goods, unless he first binds the strong man; then indeed he may plunder his house.

²⁸ "Truly, I say to you, all sins will be forgiven the sons of men, and whatever blasphemies they utter; ²⁹ but whoever blasphemes against the Holy Spirit never has forgiveness, but is guilty of an eternal sin" — ³⁰ for they had said, "He has an unclean spirit."

³¹ And his mother and his brothers came; and standing outside they sent to him and called him. ³² And a crowd was sitting about him; and they said to him, "Your mother and your brothers are outside, asking for you."

³³ And he replied, "Who are my mother and my brothers?" ³⁴ And looking around on those who sat about him, he said, "Here are my mother and my brothers! ³⁵ Whoever does the will of God is my brother, and sister, and mother."

4 Again he began to teach beside the sea. And a very large crowd gathered about him, so that he got into a boat and sat in it on the sea; and the whole crowd was beside the sea on the land. ² And he taught them many things in parables, and in his teaching he said to them: ³ "Listen! A sower went out to sow. ⁴ And as he sowed, some seed fell along the path, and the birds came and devoured it. ⁵ Other seed fell on rocky ground, where it had not much soil, and immediately it sprang up, since it had no depth of soil; ⁶ and when the sun rose it was scorched, and since it had no root it withered away. ⁷ Other seed fell among thorns and the thorns grew up and choked it, and it yielded no grain. ⁸ And other seeds fell into good soil and brought forth grain, growing up and increasing and yielding thirty-fold and sixtyfold and a hundredfold." ⁹ And he said, "He who has ears to hear, let him hear."

²⁶ And he said, "The kingdom of God is as if a man should scatter seed upon the ground, ²⁷ and should sleep and rise night and day, and the seed should sprout and grow, he knows not how. ²⁸ The earth produces of itself, first the blade, then the ear, then the full grain in the ear.

29 But when the grain is ripe, at once he puts in the sickle, because the harvest has come."

30 And he said, "With what can we compare the kingdom of God, or what parable shall we use for it? 31 It is like a grain of mustard seed, which, when sown upon the ground, is the smallest of all the seeds on earth; 32 yet when it is sown it grows up and becomes the greatest of all shrubs, and puts forth large branches, so that the birds of the air can make nests in its shade."

33 With many such parables he spoke the word to them, as they were able to hear it; 34 he did not speak to them without a parable, but privately to his own disciples he explained everything.

Teacher and Healer

SOONER or later, any popular teacher was sure to catch the attention of the authorities. Both Roman and Jewish leaders would be curious about him. This was true in Jesus' case. Soon the authorities wanted to know more about the Galilean who was causing so much excitement.

But the information they got from their spies must have been confusing. Was Jesus a harmless healer, or was he a rabble rouser? Some of the people who came to hear Jesus, seeing with their own eyes that the lame were made whole and the sick healed, cared only that he might help their bodies. Others thought he was a madman, possessed of an evil spirit. The stories Jesus told were about simple things —growing seeds and the birds of the air—but they were not always easy to understand. And at times it seemed Jesus did not even know his own family!

There were other healers in Palestine, but Jesus' powers were greater than theirs. Demons were pictured as trembling in his presence. The powers of nature—the winds, disease, even demons and death—obeyed him. Sometimes his powers worked with people who were miles away.

After a time, Jesus sent his disciples out into the country, two by two. When he sent them they, too, had the power to cast out evil spirits and heal the sick. "Repent," they said, as John the baptizer had preached before them. By this time, King Herod had executed John, and when the people said, "Jesus of Nazareth must be Elijah, come back to earth," King Herod became frightened. "No," he said, "John, whom I beheaded, has been raised."

Up to this time, Jesus had stayed in Capernaum or on the shores of the Sea of Galilee. Now he visited neighboring towns.

Mighty Works
St. Mark 4:35–41, 5:1–43, 6:1–16

4 On that day, when evening had come, he said to them, "Let us go across to the other side." ³⁶ And leaving the crowd, they took him with them, just as he was, in the boat. And other boats were with him. ³⁷ And a great storm of

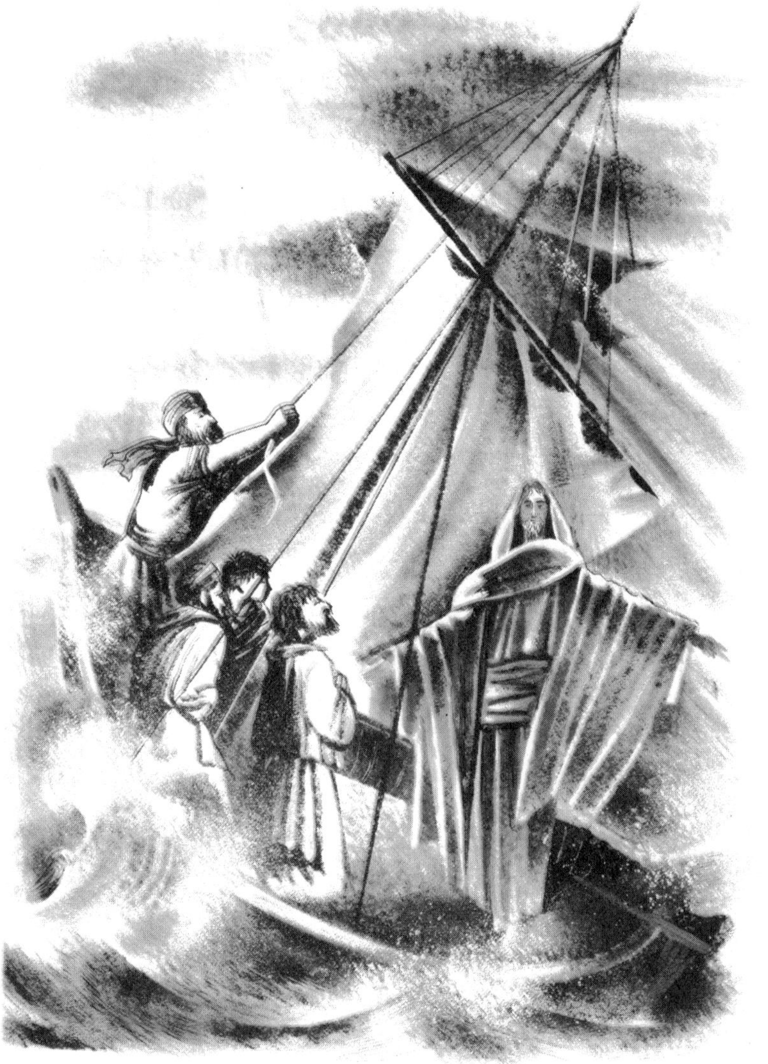

wind arose, and the waves beat into the boat, so that the boat was already filling.

38 But he was in the stern, asleep on the cushion; and they woke him and said to him, "Teacher, do you not care if we perish?"

39 And he awoke and rebuked the wind, and said to the sea, "Peace! Be still!" And the wind ceased, and there was a great calm. 40 He said to them, "Why are you afraid? Have you no faith?"

41 And they were filled with awe, and said to one another, "Who then is this, that even wind and sea obey him?"

5 They came to the other side of the sea, to the country of the Gerasenes. 2 And when he had come out of the boat, there met him out of the tombs a man with an unclean spirit, 3 who lived among the tombs; and no one could bind him any more, even with a chain; 4 for he had often been bound with fetters and chains, but the chains he wrenched apart, and the fetters he broke in pieces; and no one had the strength to subdue him. 5 Night and day among the tombs and on the mountains he was always crying out, and bruising himself with stones. 6 And when he saw Jesus from afar, he ran and worshiped him; 7 and crying out with a loud voice, he said, "What have you to do with me, Jesus, Son of the Most High God? I adjure you by God, do not torment me." 8 For he had said to him, "Come out of the man, you unclean spirit!"

9 And Jesus asked him, "What is your name?"

He replied, "My name is Legion; for we are many." ¹⁰ And he begged him eagerly not to send them out of the country. ¹¹ Now a great herd of swine was feeding there on the hillside; ¹² and they begged him, "Send us to the swine, let us enter them." ¹³ So he gave them leave. And the unclean spirits came out, and entered the swine; and the herd, numbering about two thousand, rushed down the steep bank into the sea, and were drowned in the sea.

¹⁴ The herdsmen fled, and told it in the city and in the country. And people came to see what it was that had happened. ¹⁵ And they came to Jesus, and saw the demoniac sitting there, clothed and in his right mind, the man who had had the legion; and they were afraid. ¹⁶ And those who had seen it told what had happened to the demoniac and to the swine. ¹⁷ And they began to beg Jesus to depart from their neighborhood.

¹⁸ And as he was getting into the boat, the man who had been possessed with demons begged him that he might be with him. ¹⁹ But he refused, and said to him, "Go home to your friends, and tell them how much the Lord has done for you, and how he has had mercy on you." ²⁰ And he went away and began to proclaim in the Decapolis how much Jesus had done for him; and all men marveled.

²¹ And when Jesus had crossed again in the boat to the other side, a great crowd gathered about him; and he was beside the sea. ²² Then came one of the rulers of the synagogue, Jairus by name; and seeing him, he fell at his feet, ²³ and besought him, saying, "My little daughter is at the point of death. Come and lay your hands on her, so that

she may be made well, and live." ²⁴ And he went with him.

And a great crowd followed him and thronged about him. ²⁵ And there was a woman who had had a flow of blood for twelve years, ²⁶ and who had suffered much under many physicians, and had spent all that she had, and was no better but rather grew worse. ²⁷ She had heard the reports about Jesus, and came up behind him in the crowd and touched his garment. ²⁸ For she said, "If I touch even his garments, I shall be made well." ²⁹ And immediately the hemorrhage ceased; and she felt in her body that she was healed of her disease.

³⁰ And Jesus, perceiving in himself that power had gone forth from him, immediately turned about in the crowd, and said, "Who touched my garments?"

³¹ And his disciples said to him, "You see the crowd pressing around you, and yet you say, 'Who touched me?'" ³² And he look around to see who had done it.

³³ But the woman, knowing what had been done to her, came in fear and trembling and fell down before him, and told him the whole truth. ³⁴ And he said to her, "Daughter, your faith has made you well; go in peace, and be healed of your disease."

³⁵ While he was still speaking, there came from the ruler's house some who said, "Your daughter is dead. Why trouble the Teacher any further?"

³⁶ But ignoring what they said, Jesus said to the ruler of the synagogue, "Do not fear, only believe." ³⁷ And he allowed no one to follow him except Peter and James and John the brother of James. ³⁸ When they came to the house

of the ruler of the synagogue, he saw a tumult, and people weeping and wailing loudly. ³⁹ And when he had entered, he said to them, "Why do you make a tumult and weep? The child is not dead but sleeping." ⁴⁰ And they laughed at him. But he put them all outside, and took the child's father and mother and those who were with him, and went in where the child was. ⁴¹ Taking her by the hand he said to her, "Talitha cumi"; which means, "Little girl, I say to you, arise." ⁴² And immediately the girl got up and walked; for she was twelve years old.

And immediately they were overcome with amazement. ⁴³ And he strictly charged them that no one should know this, and told them to give her something to eat.

6 He went away from there and came to his own country; and his disciples followed him. ² And on the sabbath he began to teach in the synagogue; and many who heard him were astonished, saying, "Where did this man get all this? What is the wisdom given to him? What mighty works are wrought by his hands! ³ Is not this the carpenter, the son of Mary and brother of James and Joses and Judas and Simon, and are not his sisters here with us?" And they took offense at him.

⁴ And Jesus said to them, "A prophet is not without honor, except in his own country, and among his own kin, and in his own house." ⁵ And he could do no mighty work there, except that he laid his hands upon a few sick people and healed them. ⁶ And he marveled because of their unbelief.

And he went about among the villages teaching.

⁷ And he called to him the twelve, and began to send them out two by two, and gave them authority over the unclean spirits. ⁸ He charged them to take nothing for their journey except a staff; no bread, no bag, no money in their belts; ⁹ but to wear sandals and not put on two tunics. ¹⁰ And he said to them, "Where you enter a house, stay there until you leave the place. ¹¹ And if any place will not receive you and they refuse to hear you, when you leave, shake off the dust that is on your feet for a testimony against them."

¹² So they went out and preached that men should repent. ¹³ And they cast out many demons, and anointed with oil many that were sick and healed them.

¹⁴ King Herod heard of it; for Jesus' name had become known. Some said, "John the baptizer has been raised from the dead; that is why these powers are at work in him." ¹⁵ But others said, "It is Elijah." And others said, "It is a prophet, like one of the prophets of old." ¹⁶ But when Herod heard of it he said, "John, whom I beheaded, has been raised."

Do Not Fear

THE STORIES of Jesus' healing power were enlarged as people repeated them. One of the wildest men Jesus cured, the man who lived in the mountains, among the tombs, said he was *full* of demons. As the story was passed from one to another, it grew into a tale that Jesus had sent the demons into two thousand pigs, and that the pigs immediately dove over a cliff and were drowned in the sea. Because pigs were considered "unclean" by both Jews and Jewish-Christians, this made a good story.

Jesus' family was large and well known in Nazareth. In his youth he had worked in the carpenter shop, learning a trade like any other young man. Now when he came back to his home town and preached in the synagogue, the neighbors could not take him seriously. "Why, where did Joseph and Mary's son get all that learning?" they must have asked themselves. "His brothers and sisters don't act so uppity."

It was at about this time that Jesus' ministry began to change. Before, only he had preached and healed the sick. Now he sent the disciples out by themselves to represent him. When they asked who would pay for their food and clothing, he answered as he had answered earlier in the storm at sea, "Don't worry. Don't be afraid." It was as though he were saying, "If God has important work for us to do, He will take care of us. Have faith."

Chapter 4

Feeding the Five Thousand

JOHN the baptizer was dead, and Jesus had taken his place in the imagination of the people. "Who is he?" became the great question. "A prophet," some said, and by this they meant that his teaching came straight from God. "Elijah," others said, just as they had earlier about John the baptizer. Still others had the amazing idea that Jesus was John himself come back to life. King Herod, who had unjustly put John to death, was one of these.

When people wait for a big event to happen, they make up all sorts of stories about what the great day will be like when it finally comes. This was especially true of the Jews. Because they were so oppressed, they spent lots of time talking about the Messiah and what would happen when he came to deliver them. Most people pictured the Messiah as a great warrior king, a splendid leader. Some of the more imaginative said that when God brought in His kingdom, the curse laid on the earth at the time Adam and Eve were driven from the Garden of Eden would be taken away. Then men would not have to work and sweat to make a living from the stony ground. Instead, grapes would be as large as apples, and there would be enough for everyone. Others added that the first thing which would happen when the Messiah came would be a great banquet, at which the Messiah would preside.

The coming of the Messiah, the Day of the Lord, was the last thing King Herod wanted. He knew it would mean the end of his kingdom. Herod was also scared of a revolution, or of anything his Roman overlords might interpret as a revolution. One of the reasons why Herod had arrested John the Baptist was because he feared the popular John might start a revolt.

Now Jesus had King Herod worried for the same reason. St. Luke's Gospel says that some friendly Pharisees warned Jesus that Herod planned to kill him just as he had killed John. Jesus' reply went something like this: "Go and tell that fox I still have work to do, and that he is not going to catch me before I go to Jerusalem!"

No matter where Jesus went, there were crowds, confusion, excitement, and rumors. People followed him into the country and slept in the open. But they had to eat, and there was no place to buy food. The Roman soldiers and the Jewish leaders kept a close watch on everything, for they knew that crowds have great power. They can hang a man without a trial, and they can crown a man king without an election. The rumors which spread about Jesus added to the excitement and expectation.

The people asked themselves, "What will Jesus say? Who is he really? What will he do?"

The Messiah's Banquet: *St. Mark 6:30–52*

6 The apostles returned to Jesus, and told him all that they had done and taught. ³¹ And he said to them, "Come away by yourselves to a lonely place, and rest a while." For many were coming and going, and they had no leisure even to eat. ³² And they went away in the boat to a lonely place by themselves. ³³ Now many saw them going, and knew them, and they ran there on foot from all the towns, and got there ahead of them. ³⁴ As he landed he saw a great throng, and he had compassion on them, because they were like sheep without a shepherd; and he began to teach them many things.

³⁵ And when it grew late, his disciples came to him and said, "This is a lonely place, and the hour is now late; ³⁶ send them away, to go into the country and villages round about and buy themselves something to eat."

³⁷ But he answered them, "You give them something to eat."

And they said to him, "Shall we go and buy two hundred denarii worth of bread, and give it to them to eat?"

38 And he said to them, "How many loaves have you? Go and see."

And when they had found out, they said, "Five, and two fish."

39 Then he commanded them all to sit down by companies upon the green grass. 40 So they sat down in groups, by hundreds and by fifties. 41 And taking the five loaves and the two fish he looked up to heaven, and blessed, and broke the loaves, and gave them to the disciples to set before the people; and he divided the two fish among them all. 42 And they all ate and were satisfied. 43 And they took up twelve baskets full of broken pieces and of the fish. 44 And those who ate the loaves were five thousand men.

45 Immediately he made his disciples get into the boat and go before him to the other side, to Bethsaida, while he dismissed the crowd. 46 And after he had taken leave of them, he went into the hills to pray.

47 And when evening came, the boat was out on the sea, and he was alone on the land. 48 And he saw that they were distressed in rowing, for the wind was against them.

And about the fourth watch of the night he came to them, walking on the sea. He meant to pass by them, 49 but when they saw him walking on the sea they thought it was a ghost, and cried out; 50 for they all saw him, and were terrified.

But immediately he spoke to them and said, "Take heart, it is I; have no fear." 51 And he got into the boat with them and the wind ceased. And they were utterly astounded, 52 for they did not understand about the loaves, but their hearts were hardened.

What Does It Mean?

THERE are many stories in the Old Testament in which God fed His people. The children of Israel were fed in the wilderness with manna from heaven. Elisha fed one hundred men with the gifts of one man, and food was left over. The great religious meal of Old Testament people was a thanksgiving feast held each year to celebrate the anniversary of the freeing of the Israelites from slavery in Egypt. This was called the Feast of the Passover, because the angel of death *passed over* the homes of the Israelites as they ate their final meal in Egypt before the escape. One reason the people expected a heavenly banquet when the Messiah came was because these stories were familiar to them.

Jesus taught about God's kingdom and what it was like. He had power over sickness, demons, and death. The crowds who followed him must have watched very closely for any signs that would mean the kingdom of God was at hand.

Five thousand were gathered by the shores of Galilee. It was late. They were hungry. One moment there was no food; the next there was food and to spare for all. St. John's Gospel says that the people tried to crown Jesus king on the spot, but he escaped into the hills. St. Mark also suggests that some such thing might have happened, since Jesus forced the disciples to leave the scene in great haste: "Immediately he made his disciples get into the boat and go before him to the other side, to Bethsaida, while he dismissed the crowd." It may be the disciples were among those who were trying to crown Jesus king. When he came to them in the boat they still did not understand that he was God's special messenger. They were as unimpressionable as though their hearts had been made of stone.

Private Lessons

THE CROWDS had followed Jesus when he tried to take the disciples to a lonely spot to be with them alone. Soon after the great feeding, Jesus took the twelve away. They visited a number of places north and west of Galilee. During this period, Jesus had more time to be with his disciples. Now he could explain more fully some of the mystery of who the Messiah really was.

Gathering Up the Crumbs: *St. Mark 7:24–37*

7 And from there he arose and went away to the region of Tyre and Sidon. And he entered a house, and would not have any one know it; yet he could not be hid. [25] But immediately a woman, whose little daughter was possessed by an unclean spirit, heard of him, and came and fell down at his feet. [26] Now the woman was a Greek, a Syrophoenician by birth. And she begged him to cast the demon out of her daughter. [27] And he said to her, "Let the children first be fed, for it is not right to take the children's bread and throw it to the dogs."

²⁸ But she answered him, "Yes, Lord; yet even the dogs under the table eat the children's crumbs."

²⁹ And he said to her, "For this saying you may go your way; the demon has left your daughter." ³⁰ And she went home, and found the child lying in bed, and the demon gone.

³¹ Then he returned from the region of Tyre, and went through Sidon to the Sea of Galilee, through the region of the Decapolis. ³² And they brought to him a man who was deaf and had an impediment in his speech; and they besought him to lay his hand upon him. ³³ And taking him aside from the multitude privately, he put his fingers into his ears, and he spat and touched his tongue; ³⁴ and looking up to heaven, he sighed, and said to him, "Ephphatha," that is, "Be opened." ³⁵ And his ears were opened, his tongue was released, and he spoke plainly.

³⁶ And he charged them to tell no one; but the more he charged them, the more zealously they proclaimed it. ³⁷ And they were astonished beyond measure, saying, "He has done all things well; he even makes the deaf hear and the dumb speak."

Jesus Among the Gentiles

THE DISCIPLES seemed as blind as a blind man. They were extremely dense, for they had more opportunity to understand Jesus than the crowds did. Even though the people who followed Jesus in Galilee did not know who he was, they appreciated and honored him. The evil spirits always seemed to recognize him. It was almost as though only the specially chosen disciples did not understand.

When Jesus went outside Jewish territory to Tyre and Sidon, forty-five miles west on the coast of the Mediterranean Sea, "he could not be hid," says St. Mark. A complete stranger, a Syrian woman from Phoenicia who spoke only Greek, came to him for help. Jesus tested her faith and then cured her daughter without even going to see the child.

St. Mark is careful to describe how people felt about Jesus. Back in Capernaum the wondering crowd had exclaimed, "We never saw anything like this!" Now, from the lips of non-Jews, came the same kind of wonder and awe: "He has done all things well; he even makes the deaf hear and the dumb speak." These Gentiles were using almost the same words that the prophet Isaiah had used when he described what would take place on the great Day of the Lord:

"Then the eyes of the blind shall be opened, and
the ears of the deaf unstopped . . . " (Isa. 35:5)

The disciples certainly were familiar with Old Testament prophecies. Every Jew knew them. Could they not put two and two together? Were the Gentiles smarter than they? Or were the twelve so close to Jesus that they could not recognize him for what he was?

Chapter 5

Who Is He?

JESUS and his twelve disciples had been away from the large and excited crowds for some time. The disciples had had a chance to know and understand him better. Now it was time to test their knowledge and their faith in him. He did so near the city of Caesarea Philippi.

Shortly after, Jesus took Peter, James, and John with him to a quiet mountain slope. Here, probably on a high spur of Mount Hermon, fourteen miles north of Caesarea Philippi, these three disciples gained new understanding about what the Messiah meant. St. Mark says, Jesus "was transfigured before them."

Peter Is Right: Peter Is Wrong
St. Mark 8:27–38; 9:2–13

8 And Jesus went on with his disciples, to the villages of Caesarea Philippi; and on the way he asked his disciples, "Who do men say that I am?"

28 And they told him, "John the Baptist; and others say, Elijah; and others one of the prophets."

29 And he asked them, "But who do you say that I am?" Peter answered him, "You are the Christ."

30 And he charged them to tell no one about him.

31 And he began to teach them that the Son of man must suffer many things, and be rejected by the elders and the chief priests and the scribes, and be killed, and after three days rise again. 32 And he said this plainly.

And Peter took him, and began to rebuke him.

33 But turning and seeing his disciples, he rebuked Peter, and said, "Get behind me, Satan! For you are not on the side of God, but of men."

34 And he called to him the multitude with his disciples, and said to them, "If any man would come after me, let him deny himself and take up his cross and follow me. 35 For whoever would save his life will lose it; and whoever loses his life for my sake and the gospel's will save it. 36 For what does it profit a man, to gain the whole world and forfeit his life? 37 For what can a man give in return for his life? 38 For whoever is ashamed of me and of my words in this adulterous and sinful generation, of him will the Son

of man also be ashamed, when he comes in the glory of his Father with the holy angels."

9 And after six days Jesus took with him Peter and James and John, and led them up a high mountain apart by themselves; and he was transfigured before them, ³ and his garments became glistening, intensely white, as no fuller on earth could bleach them. ⁴ And there appeared to them Elijah with Moses; and they were talking to Jesus.

⁵ And Peter said to Jesus, "Master, it is well that we are here; let us make three booths, one for you and one for Moses and one for Elijah." ⁶ For he did not know what to say, for they were exceedingly afraid.

⁷ And a cloud overshadowed them, and a voice came out of the cloud, "This is my beloved Son; listen to him." ⁸ And suddenly looking around they no longer saw any one with them but Jesus only.

⁹ And as they were coming down the mountain, he charged them to tell no one what they had seen, until the Son of man should have risen from the dead. ¹⁰ So they kept the matter to themselves, questioning what the rising from the dead meant.

¹¹ And they asked him, "Why do the scribes say that first Elijah must come?"

¹² And he said to them, "Elijah does come first to restore all things; and how is it written of the Son of man, that he should suffer many things and be treated with contempt? ¹³ But I tell you that Elijah has come, and they did to him whatever they pleased, as it is written of him."

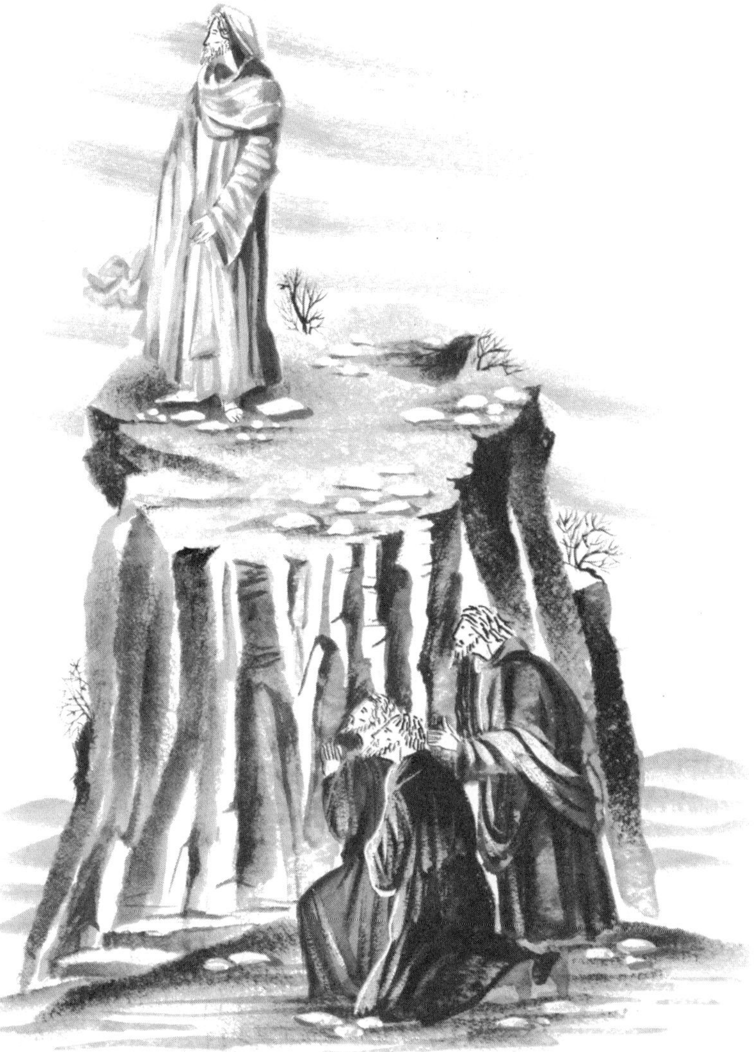

God's Beloved Son

CHRIST is the Greek word for *Messiah,* and it means "the anointed one." Peter's answer, "You are the Christ," is known as "Peter's confession." The word *confess* in this sense means "say for yourself."

One would think that Peter, at least, truly understood who Jesus was. But it soon became clear that Peter's understanding of the meaning of *Messiah* was quite different from Jesus' idea. When Jesus began to tell the twelve that he, the Messiah, must suffer many things and be rejected and killed, Peter argued and even reproved Jesus: "You can't let this happen to you!" he said.

In explaining what was going to happen, Jesus used a new term, "the Son of man." The prophet Daniel told how a heavenly being "like a son of man" was given power to rule His kingdom by God. (Dan. 7:12–14) So "Son of man" really means "the heavenly Son of God." In explaining the Scriptures to his disciples, Jesus said that the Son of man was like the servant of God described in the Book of Isaiah (Isa. 53). He must suffer *before* he was glorified and given the kingdom.

This was almost a new interpretation of the Scriptures. The Jews thought their awaited Messiah would triumph right from the beginning, and triumph in the sense of being strong and successful, perhaps a warrior king like David. He might even come on the clouds of heaven. Peter and his fellow disciples did not understand their rabbi any better than the crowds who longed for a king. When Peter insisted that Jesus must not suffer, his voice was to Jesus like the voice of Satan, tempting Jesus not to follow the way God expected him to take.

A week later, Peter, James, and John had an experience which strengthened their faith. The vision they saw when they went to Mount Hermon with Jesus had a special, wonderful meaning.

The sparkling white clothes were a sign to them that Jesus was truly the Son of God. The two visitors were Moses, the great prophet, and Elijah, the one who would come just before the Messiah. These two stood for Israel's great past. The fact that Jesus was seen talking with them was very important. Then the cloud hid them from view, and only Jesus remained.

A cloud to the Jews was a sign of God's glorious presence. The three disciples heard a voice out of the cloud. God's voice said, "This is my beloved Son; listen to him." What had been Jesus' secret at his baptism was now known to three of his disciples. He asked them to keep his secret until after the Resurrection.

Even now the three disciples were only partly aware of what was going to happen. Jesus predicted that he would suffer, be treated with contempt, and finally rise from the dead, but although they were overwhelmed by their vision, they still did not see clearly.

Carrying the Vision to Men

JESUS and the three disciples could not stay on the mountain. They had to return to the world of men, and there they had to face misunderstanding. Praying must have been easy in the presence of the great figures of the Old Testament, where God was as close as the fog. Prayer is harder when there are no visions, where men suffer and have doubts. But Jesus and his followers were needed among the sinful and suffering people who always aroused his compassion.

Help My Unbelief: *St. Mark 9:14–41*

9 And when they came to the disciples, they saw a great crowd about them, and scribes arguing with them. 15 And immediately all the crowd, when they saw him, were greatly amazed, and ran up to him and greeted him.

16 And he asked them, "What are you discussing with them?"

17 And one of the crowd answered him, "Teacher, I brought my son to you, for he has a dumb spirit; 18 and wherever it seizes him, it dashes him down; and he foams and grinds his teeth and becomes rigid; and I asked your disciples to cast it out, and they were not able."

19 And he answered them, "O faithless generation, how long am I to be with you? How long am I to bear with

you? Bring him to me." 20 And they brought the boy to him; and when the spirit saw him, immediately it convulsed the boy, and he fell on the ground and rolled about, foaming at the mouth.

21 And Jesus asked his father, "How long has he had this?"

And he said, "From childhood. 22 And it has often cast him into the fire and into the water, to destroy him; but if you can do anything, have pity on us and help us."

23 And Jesus said to him, "If you can! All things are possible to him who believes."

24 Immediately the father of the child cried out and said, "I believe; help my unbelief!"

25 And when Jesus saw that a crowd came running together, he rebuked the unclean spirit, saying to it, "You dumb and deaf spirit, I command you, come out of him, and never enter him again."

26 And after crying out and convulsing him terribly, it came out, and the boy was like a corpse; so that most of them said, "He is dead." 27 But Jesus took him by the hand and lifted him up, and he arose.

28 And when he had entered the house, his disciples asked him privately, "Why could we not cast it out?"

29 And he said to them "This kind cannot be driven out by anything but prayer."

30 They went on from there and passed through Galilee. And he would not have any one know it; 31 for he was teaching his disciples, saying to them, "The Son of man will be delivered into the hands of men, and they will kill

him; and when he is killed, after three days he will rise." ³² But they did not understand the saying, and they were afraid to ask him.

³³ And they came to Capernaum; and when he was in the house he asked them, "What were you discussing on the way?" ³⁴ But they were silent; for on the way they had discussed with one another who was the greatest. ³⁵ And he sat down and called the twelve; and he said to them, "If any one would be first, he must be last of all and servant of all." ³⁶ And he took a child, and put him in the midst of them; and taking him in his arms, he said to them, ³⁷ "Whoever receives one such child in my name receives me; and whoever receives me, receives not me but him who sent me."

³⁸ John said to him, "Teacher, we saw a man casting out demons in your name, and we forbade him, because he was not following us."

³⁹ But Jesus said, "Do not forbid him; for no one who does a mighty work in my name will be able soon after to speak evil of me. ⁴⁰ For he that is not against us is for us. ⁴¹ For truly, I say to you, whoever gives you a cup of water to drink because you bear the name of Christ, will by no means lose his reward."

Special Help

JESUS now had an obvious single purpose. He was trying to help his disciples come to a fuller understanding of who he was and what was going to happen. Peter failed to understand the first time he heard Jesus' explanation, although Peter had been excited when he confessed, "You are the Christ!" A week later, after the vision on the mountain, Jesus told the disciples again who he was. Even a third time he told them, and it must have been heartbreaking that they could not catch his meaning.

There was an urgency in what Jesus said and did. There was a sense of suppressed excitement, a whisper of great and important events soon to come. He spent more time with the disciples, for it was they who would have to carry out his mission. King Herod might arrest him before he finished his work. Jesus had no time to lose. Time was running out on him.

One effect of Jesus' attempt to teach his disciples about coming events was that they began to act very self-important. They were convinced, now, that Jesus was going to do something to bring in the kingdom. They tried to keep those outside the group from casting out demons in Jesus' name. They argued among themselves about who was the greatest among them. They attempted to keep little children away from Jesus. They were thinking of earthly power and of themselves as officers!

Chapter 6

The Challenge

JESUS now left Galilee to go into Judea. In Judea he was out of King Herod's territory, since Judea was governed directly by a Roman governor.

Was this a safer place? Hardly. The principal city of Judea was Jerusalem, the home of the Temple and of the chief priests. These priests were the protectors of the Jewish religion. Jerusalem was also the headquarters of the Pharisees, the champions of the Law of Moses, and some of them were Jesus' old enemies. The Roman official responsible for law and order was the procurator, Pontius Pilate, whose main job was to rule peaceably and to avoid trouble at any cost.

THE CHALLENGE · 63

Jerusalem was the center of the world for every Jew. The heart of the life of the city was the Temple, the only place where sacrifices of animals and birds could be made. It was the symbol of the religious and political hopes of the nation.

Jerusalem was the largest city in Palestine, and it always had many visitors. Every pious Jew was determined to make at least one pilgrimage there during his lifetime, and the favorite period of the year was when a great religious festival was scheduled. Often the city was so crowded that people slept on the open ground.

In the spring, when the feast of the Passover was approaching, Jesus started to Jerusalem. He knew that he would be opposed, for in Jerusalem were the real rulers of the people. Under the Jewish form of government, the high priests acted as head of both Temple and state, although Pontius Pilate controlled the military force, the Roman army.

The high priest was helped by his chief priests and by a council of seventy-one called the Sanhedrin. The members of this council were chief priests, rich merchants, leading scribes, and a few other Pharisees. The Sanhedrin had some freedom, chiefly in religious matters.

The Romans had things well in hand. They could work through the Sanhedrin and according to Jewish customs, and this kept the people reasonably happy. But the Romans were always ready to step in if anything went wrong. They always had control of the army, the courts, and taxes.

What Jesus taught of the rule of God threatened both

Roman and Jewish leaders. Talk of another king or kingdom meant to the Romans the threat of rebellion. The huge crowds who followed Jesus looked like rabble to them, and the Roman authorities were on the alert. If the Jews could not handle this rabble rouser, the Romans would have to step in. Unless the Jewish leaders in Judea put a stop to Jesus and his work, they were likely to find themselves in very serious trouble with the Roman authorities and lose their own power.

Most of the Jewish authorities approved of their alliance with Rome, and life in Judea was peaceful and prosperous for those in high positions. But Jesus' ministry also threatened them religiously. The high priest and his followers were the real authorities in the field of religion. If God's agent, His Messiah, had really come, they would have been the first to know and proclaim it, they reasoned. And yet nobody had the right to say or do what Jesus had been saying and doing in Galilee, unless he really was the agent of God.

The Jewish authorities could not afford to admit that Jesus had the right to say or do these things. In the first place, he came from Nazareth in Galilee, a district in which strict Jewish practices were often ignored. Second, the high priest and the Sanhedrin did not recognize him as an authority in religious matters. Third, he did not act like the kind of Messiah they thought the Old Testament foretold.

Before arriving in Jerusalem, where the showdown with his enemies would take place, Jesus had more chances to heal and to teach. As he came through Judea, he attracted great crowds just as he had in Galilee. And during this time, Jesus still tried to get his disciples ready for the test which was coming.

Hard Questions: Harder Answers
St. Mark 10:1–45

10 And he left there and went to the region of Judea and beyond the Jordan, and crowds gathered to him again; and again, as his custom was, he taught them.

2 And Pharisees came up and in order to test him asked, "Is it lawful for a man to divorce his wife?"

3 He answered them, "What did Moses command you?"

4 They said, "Moses allowed a man to write a certificate of divorce, and to put her away."

5 But Jesus said to them, "For your hardness of heart he wrote you this commandment. 6 But from the beginning of creation, 'God made them male and female.' 7 'For this reason a man shall leave his father and mother and be joined to his wife, 8 and the two shall become one.' So they are no longer two but one. 9 What therefore God has joined together, let not man put asunder."

10 And in the house the disciples asked him again about this matter. 11 And he said to them, "Whoever divorces his wife and marries another, commits adultery against her; 12 and if she divorces her husband and marries another, she commits adultery."

¹³ And they were bringing children to him, that he might touch them; and the disciples rebuked them. ¹⁴ But when Jesus saw it he was indignant, and said to them, "Let the children come to me, do not hinder them; for to such belongs the kingdom of God. ¹⁵ Truly, I say to you, whoever does not receive the kingdom of God like a child shall not enter it." ¹⁶ And he took them in his arms and blessed them, laying his hands upon them.

¹⁷ And as he was setting out on his journey, a man ran up and knelt before him, and asked him, "Good Teacher, what must I do to inherit eternal life?"

¹⁸ And Jesus said to him, "Why do you call me good? No one is good but God alone. ¹⁹ You know the commandments: 'Do not kill, Do not commit adultery, Do not steal, Do not bear false witness, Do not defraud, Honor your father and mother.'"

²⁰ And he said to him, "Teacher, all these I have observed from my youth."

²¹ And Jesus looking upon him loved him, and said to him, "You lack one thing; go, sell what you have, and give it to the poor, and you will have treasure in heaven; and come, follow me."

²² At that saying his countenance fell, and he went away sorrowful; for he had great possessions.

²³ And Jesus looked around and said to his disciples, "How hard it will be for those who have riches to enter the kingdom of God!" ²⁴ And the disciples were amazed at his words. But Jesus said to them again, "Children, how hard it is to enter the kingdom of God! ²⁵ It is easier for a

camel to go through the eye of a needle than for a rich man to enter the kingdom of God."

26 And they were exceedingly astonished, and said to him, "Then who can be saved?"

27 Jesus looked at them and said, "With men it is impossible, but not with God; for all things are possible with God."

28 Peter began to say to him, "Lo, we have left everything and followed you."

29 Jesus said, "Truly, I say to you, there is no one who has left house or brothers or sisters or mother or father or children or lands, for my sake and for the gospel, 30 who will not receive a hundredfold now in this time, houses and brothers and sisters and mothers and children and lands, with persecutions, and in the age to come eternal life. 31 But many that are first will be last, and the last first."

32 And they were on the road, going up to Jerusalem, Jesus was walking ahead of them; and they were amazed, and those who followed were afraid. And taking the twelve again, he began to tell them what was to happen to him, 33 saying, "Behold, we are going up to Jerusalem; and the Son of man will be delivered to the chief priests and the scribes, and they will condemn him to death, and deliver him to the Gentiles; 34 and they will mock him, and spit upon him, and scourge him, and kill him; and after three days he will rise."

35 And James and John, the sons of Zebedee, came forward to him, and said to him, "Teacher, we want you to do for us whatever we ask of you."

[36] And he said to them, "What do you want me to do for you?"

[37] And they said to him, "Grant us to sit, one at your right hand and one at your left, in your glory."

[38] But Jesus said to them, "You do not know what you are asking. Are you able to drink the cup that I drink, or to be baptized with the baptism with which I am baptized?"

[39] And they said to him, "We are able."

And Jesus said to them, "The cup that I drink you will drink; and with the baptism with which I am baptized, you will be baptized; [40] but to sit at my right hand or at my left is not mine to grant, but it is for those for whom it has been prepared."

[41] And when the ten heard it, they began to be indignant at James and John.

[42] And Jesus called them to him and said to them, "You know that those who are supposed to rule over the Gentiles lord it over them, and their great men exercise authority over them. [43] But it shall not be so among you; but whoever would be great among you must be your servant, [44] and whoever would be first among you must be slave of all. [45] For the Son of man also came not to be served but to serve, and to give his life as a ransom for many."

The Gift of the Kingdom

JUST after Jesus had said that the kingdom of God is something to be *received,* as a child receives or accepts a gift he has not earned, a man came up and, with a great show of reverence, asked, "Good Teacher, what must I do to inherit eternal life?" The man wanted to earn and to deserve entrance into the kingdom of God. He believed, with the Pharisees, that one is saved by obedience to the Law. But Jesus said to him, "No one is *good* but God alone." No man is good enough to deserve salvation, but with God it is possible. God draws us to Him, but we cannot *earn* a new relationship with Him.

Then Peter asked a question which shows how slowly he was learning, how hard it was to change the ideas he had held for so long a time. Peter wanted to be assured that at least the twelve had earned their way into the kingdom. "Lo, we have left *everything* and followed you," he said. Jesus promised them that they would be rewarded a hundred times over. He did not mean that they would have a hundred wives, a hundred mothers and fathers, but that there would be such warmth and companionship in the fellowship of the disciples that they would be rewarded a hundred times over.

This fellowship was not a matter of political power; arguments over who would hold the highest position were silly. Earthly rulers like to lord it over their people, but the disciples must learn to be servants, Jesus was saying. Even the Son of man came to serve others, and to give his life for many.

As Jesus walked on toward Jerusalem, the disciples were both amazed and afraid. He tried to tell them what to expect, and it slowly began to dawn on them that they might have to share in his suffering.

Seeing and Not Seeing

JERUSALEM meant danger! Yet Jesus seemed to be drawn, as if by a magnet, toward the city. Since the day of the vision on Mount Hermon, Jesus' purpose was more certain.

Jesus and his followers had arrived at Jericho, in the territory of Judea, the last stopping place in the eighty-mile journey from the shore of Galilee to Jerusalem. They were only fifteen miles from Jerusalem, and they were facing a long, dusty, up-hill walk that would take five more hours. The disciples could sense the danger to come, but they saw no sign of fear on the face of the Master. They were jostled by the people on the crowded roads as they mingled with the pilgrims walking along in a slow-moving traffic jam toward the Holy City for the Feast of the Passover. Robbers lurked in the hills. The number of beggars had greatly increased.

Jerusalem did not come into sight until almost the last few minutes of their journey, for the Mount of Olives, about two miles east of the city wall, hid it from view. Then one of the first things that Jesus and his disciples could see was the Temple building itself. The east wall, facing the rising sun each morning, was covered with plates of shining gold. Its towers or pinnacles were 180 feet high. How magnificently it stood there! And yet it was soon to be destroyed by the Romans.

Surrounding the hill on which the Temple stood, but

lower down, was the wall that enclosed the Court of the Men of Israel and the Court of the Women. Lower still was the great wall surrounding the Court of the Gentiles. The hillside then dropped sharply to the Kidron ravine, which the pilgrims had to cross.

Twice during that memorable, all-day mountain climb, Jesus' followers had an opportunity to see more clearly who he was.

Entering Jerusalem
St. Mark 10:46–52; 11:1–11

10 And they came to Jericho; and as he was leaving Jericho with his disciples and a great multitude, Bartimaeus, a blind beggar, the son of Timaeus, was sitting by the roadside. ⁴⁷ And when he heard that it was Jesus of Nazareth, he began to cry out and say, "Jesus, Son of David, have mercy on me!" ⁴⁸ And many rebuked him, telling him to be silent; but he cried out all the more, "Son of David, have mercy on me!"

⁴⁹ And Jesus stopped and said, "Call him."

And they called the blind man, saying to him, "Take heart; rise, he is calling you." ⁵⁰ And throwing off his mantle he sprang up and came to Jesus.

⁵¹ And Jesus said to him, "What do you want me to do for you?"

And the blind man said to him, "Master, let me receive my sight."

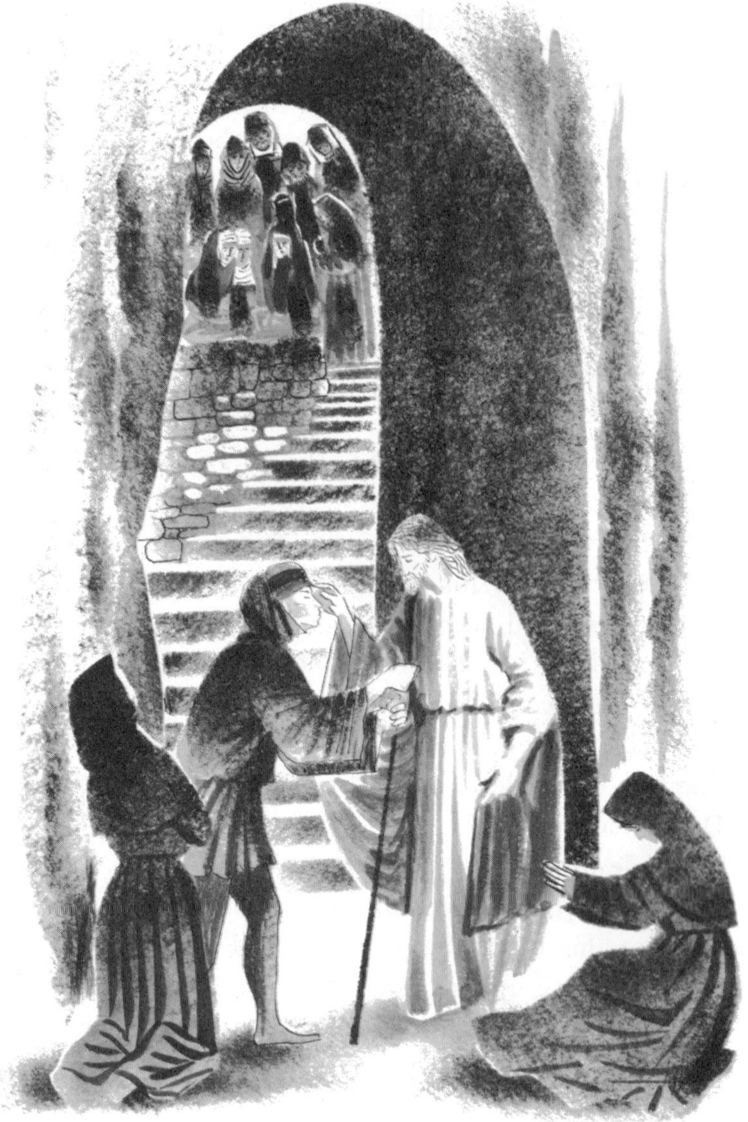

⁵² And Jesus said to him, "Go your way; your faith has made you well."

And immediately he received his sight and followed him on the way.

11 And when they drew near to Jerusalem, to Bethphage and Bethany, at the Mount of Olives, he sent two of his disciples, ² and said to them, "Go into the village opposite you, and immediately as you enter it you will find a colt tied, on which no one has ever sat; untie it and bring it. ³ If any one says to you 'Why are you doing this?' say, 'The Lord has need of it and will send it back here immediately.'"

⁴ And they went away, and found a colt tied at the door out in the open street; and they untied it. ⁵ And those who stood there said to them, "What are you doing, untying the colt?" ⁶ And they told them what Jesus had said; and they let them go. ⁷ And they brought the colt to Jesus, and threw their garments on it; and he sat upon it. ⁸ And many spread their garments on the road, and others spread leafy branches which they had cut from the fields.

⁹ And those who went before and those who followed cried out, "Hosanna! Blessed be he who comes in the name of the Lord! ¹⁰ Blessed be the kingdom of our father David that is coming! Hosanna in the highest!"

¹¹ And he entered Jerusalem, and went into the temple; and when he had looked round at everything, as it was already late, he went out to Bethany with the twelve.

The Prophecy Fulfilled

As Jesus left Jericho, a blind beggar cried out repeatedly, "Jesus, Son of David, have mercy on me!" In the crowd there were some who had heard Jesus preach and who had witnessed his healings. They were ready to believe he deserved the title "Son of David," which was one of the titles for the Messiah used by those who expected the Messiah to be a warrior king. Perhaps some of them had been among the five thousand who were fed at Galilee and who wanted to make Jesus king on the spot. So they were stirred up again when blind Bartimaeus shouted, "Son of David." Then, when Jesus healed the blind man, they became even more excited. They remembered that the prophets said a sign of the presence of the Messiah would be that the blind received their sight. No wonder the crowd became so noisy in front of the gate when they arrived at Jerusalem!

At a nearby village, Jesus had two of his disciples get a young donkey colt which had never been ridden. To the Jews, a sacred purpose required the use of something which was new. By riding on the donkey, Jesus wanted to call attention to the prophecy of Zechariah (9:9-10).

> "Rejoice greatly, O daughter of Zion!
> Shout aloud, O daughter of Jerusalem!
> Lo, your king comes to you;
> triumphant and victorious is he,

    humble and riding on an ass,
        on a colt the foal of an ass.
    I will cut off the chariot from Ephraim
        and the war horse from Jerusalem;
    and the battle bow shall be cut off,
        and he shall command peace to the nations;
    his dominion shall be from sea to sea,
        and from the River to the ends of the earth."

From another prophecy of Zechariah, many people expected that the Messiah would first appear on the Mount of Olives. And the prophet Malachi had said that the Lord would suddenly come to the Temple.

By riding on the lowly animal of peace, rather than by appearing as a conqueror, Jesus called attention to himself; but he was also saying no to the idea that he was a warrior king. His entry caused a commotion. The crowd called out loudly, "Hosanna." "God save Him!" "God bless the one who comes in the name of the Lord!" "Hurrah!" (The ancient greeting "hosanna" means "save now." It is from Psalm 118:25–26.)

To some of the pilgrims, this was just part of the excitement of going to Jerusalem. Something was always happening, but they did not stop to ask its meaning. A few may still have thought Jesus was going to lead a revolution. Even the disciples were not sure what was going to happen, but their beloved Master was showing that he was a leader! They had high hopes for Jesus and for themselves!

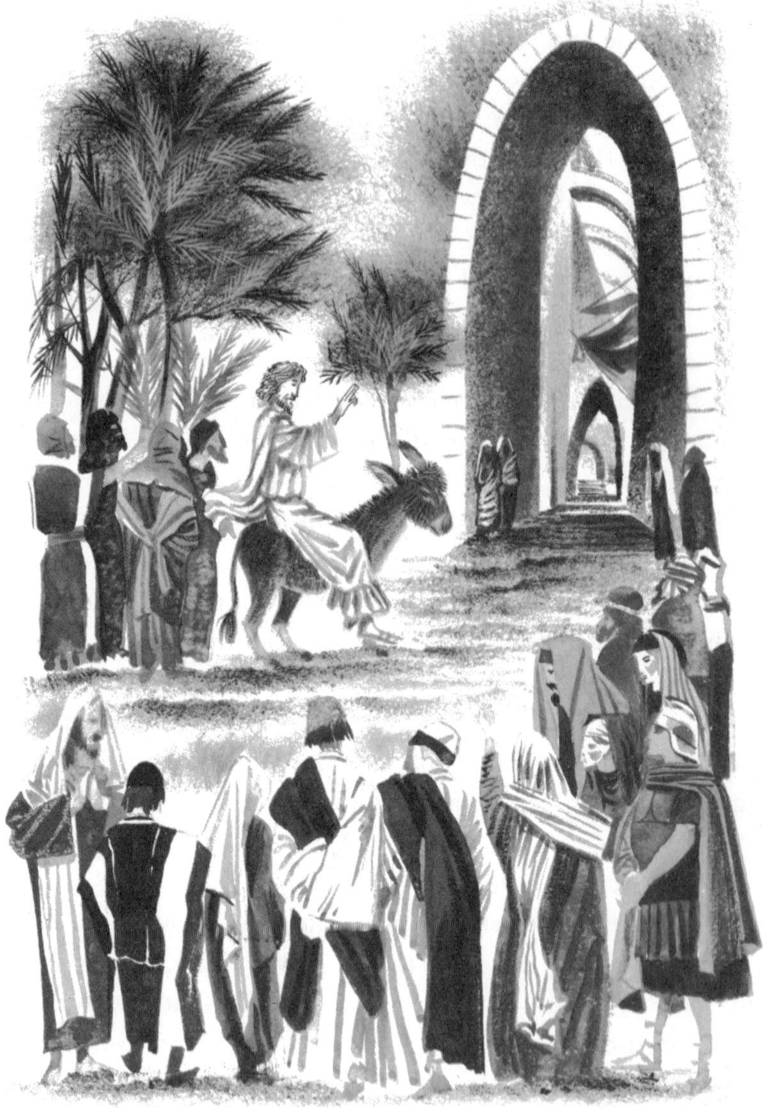

But if no one else understood, Jesus knew what he was doing. He was acting out the old prophecy of Zechariah, and he knew now that only through suffering and death would his mission be accomplished. He was ready to face pain and death. So it is we sing in Hymn 64:

> Ride on! ride on in majesty!
> In lowly pomp ride on *to die;*
> Bow thy meek head to mortal pain,
> Then take, O God, thy power, and reign.

It was done. The great step had been made, and Jesus was in the midst of his enemies. He had said, as clearly as he could act it out from the old prophecy, that he was the Messiah, but that he was a new kind of Messiah. He was the Christ long expected, and yet he was the kind of Christ that no one expected. The followers of Jesus still had much to learn. Although they may have been filled with fears, they clearly did not understand.

Jesus may have camped near Bethany that night with the twelve, for there he would be safe from his enemies.

Chapter 7

Jesus Meets His Enemies

LIFE in Jerusalem centered in the Temple and its worship. But the Temple was a strange, hard-to-understand, even disappointing place to visitors, especially if they were not Jews. The great outer court of the Temple was known as the Court of the Gentiles because it was the only part of the Temple area to which non-Jews were admitted.

Running around the inside of the wall was a long covered porch. This porch was used by leading rabbis as a gathering place for their disciples. It was "the university of Jerusalem," and between each pair of pillars that held up the porch roof was a "classroom."

In contrast to this school-like atmosphere, sheep were

tied out in the center of the court, and there were crates of pigeons or doves for sale to anyone who intended to offer a sacrifice. The Temple rules required that an animal or bird to be sacrificed must be unblemished—perfect to look at, with no injuries or scars. It was almost impossible to drive a sheep all the way from Galilee, say, or Idumea, without a scratch, so in one sense it was a real convenience for the pilgrims to have available unblemished animals and birds right in the Temple court, even though the prices were always high.

Because the priests could easily refuse to accept for sacrifice animals which had not been bought from the Temple market, what had started as a help to the visitors had become a "racket." The family of the high priest often controlled this selling, and frequently did so for private profit.

There were also booths in the Temple for moneychangers. Every adult male Jew had to pay an annual tax to the Temple of a half-shekel. Roman coins carried Caesar's image, and Jews did not think it reverent to offer them to God. So visitors with Roman money exchanged it for special Temple coins. This, too, was run for a profit that benefited the chief priests.

The Temple courtyards and the Temple buildings occupied the ridge between the north and south sides of the old city. People had come to use the Court of the Gentiles as a shortcut if they had merchandise to carry from one section of the city to the other. This added to the noise and confusion, which was already great enough with the bleating of the sheep and the arguments of the traders. Most of these people had no concern at all for the real purpose of the Temple, which was the daily worship of God.

Some Gentiles had come to believe in the God of Israel. The only place where they could pray was this noisy Court of the Gentiles. They could not go into the quieter, inner court to worship, for beside the gate which led to that inner, more sacred part of the Temple was a sign which said, "No foreigner may enter within this enclosure. Whoever is caught will be responsible for the death which overtakes him."

Many of the Jews were not happy with the noise and confusion in the outer part of the Temple, but, as in the case of the moneychangers, the chief priests had control of the situation.

Cleansing the Temple: *St. Mark 11:15–19*

11 And they came to Jerusalem. And he entered the temple and began to drive out those who sold and those who bought in the temple, and he overturned the tables of the money changers and the seats of those who sold pigeons; [16] and he would not allow any one to carry anything through the temple. [17] And he taught, and said to them, "Is it not written, 'My house shall be called a house of prayer for all the nations'? But you have made it a den of robbers." [18] And the chief priests and the scribes heard it and sought a way to destroy him; for they feared him, because all the multitude was astonished at his teaching. [19] And when evening came they went out of the city.

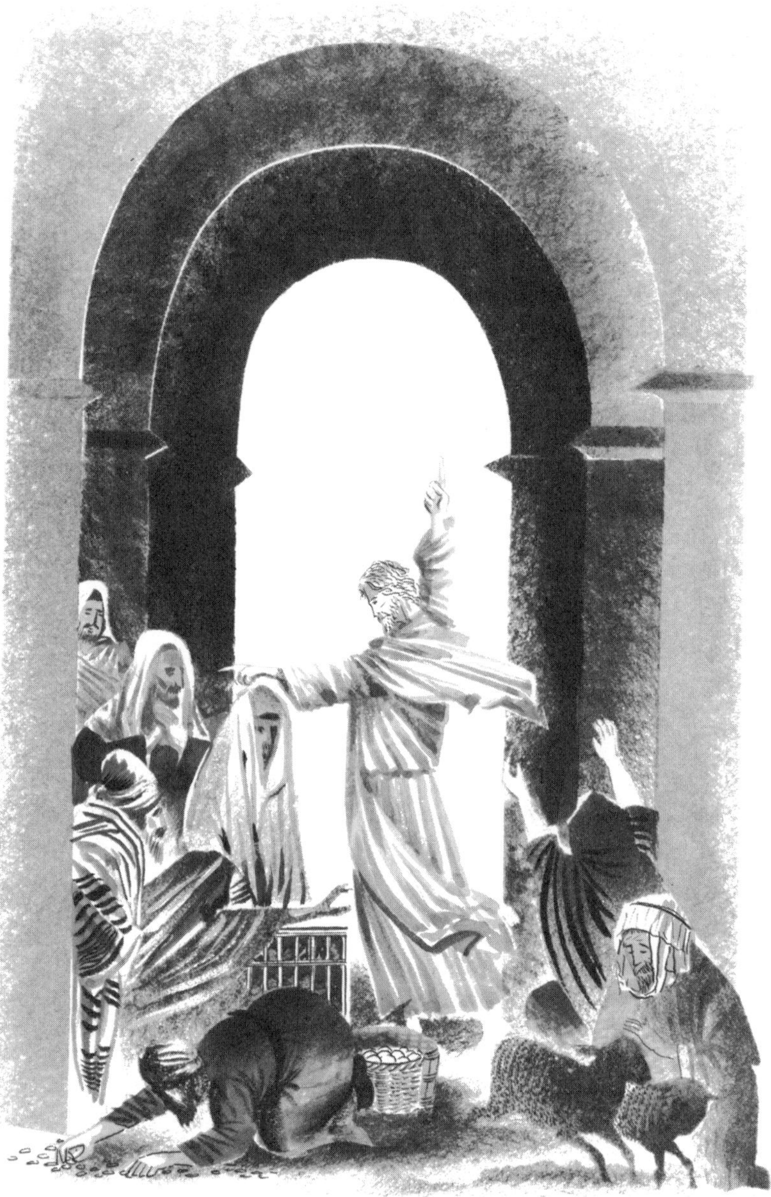

His Enemies Begin to Close In

TROUBLE was brewing fast. Jesus actually was daring his enemies to fight! Riding into the Holy City like an ancient, peace-loving king amid shouts of "Hosanna to the Son of David," he had shocked the religious authorities and had made the Romans suspect a revolt. He had criticized the way the priests were running the Temple and had therefore made them angry. When he had upset their dishonest schemes for making money from the pilgrims, they had become even more angry. Is there any wonder that they questioned his right to do such a thing? Is there any wonder that they listened carefully to his teaching? If they could trap him into making a fool of himself, that would be well and good. If they could catch him saying something illegal so that he could be arrested, that would be so much the better.

Jesus knew he had many enemies. He knew they wanted to get him in trouble, to shut him up, to get rid of him.

Battle of Words
St. Mark 11:27–33; 12:1–44; 13:1–2

11 And they came again to Jerusalem. And as he was walking in the temple, the chief priests and the scribes and the elders came to him, [28] and they said to him,

"By what authority are you doing these things, or who gave you this authority to do them?" ²⁹ Jesus said to them, "I will ask you a question; answer me, and I will tell you by what authority I do these things. ³⁰ Was the baptism of John from heaven or from men? Answer me."

³¹ And they argued with one another, "If we say, 'From heaven,' he will say, 'Why then did you not believe him?' ³² But shall we say, 'From men'?"—they were afraid of the people, for all held that John was a real prophet. ³³ So they answered Jesus, "We do not know."

And Jesus said to them, "Neither will I tell you by what authority I do these things."

12 And he began to speak to them in parables. "A man planted a vineyard, and set a hedge around it, and dug a pit for the wine press, and built a tower, and let it out to tenants, and went into another country. ² When the time came, he sent a servant to the tenants, to get from them some of the fruit of the vineyard. ³ And they took him and beat him, and sent him away empty-handed. ⁴ Again he sent to them another servant, and they wounded him in the head, and treated him shamefully. ⁵ And he sent another, and him they killed; and so with many others, some they beat and some they killed. ⁶ He had still one other, a beloved son; finally he sent him to them, saying, 'They will respect my son.' ⁷ But those tenants said to one another, 'This is the heir; come, let us kill him, and the inheritance will be ours.' ⁸ And they took him and killed him, and cast

him out of the vineyard. ⁹ What will the owner of the vineyard do? He will come and destroy the tenants, and give the vineyard to others. ¹⁰ Have you not read this scripture:

> 'The very stone which the builders rejected
> has become the head of the corner;
> ¹¹ this was the Lord's doing,
> and it is marvelous in our eyes'?"

¹² And they tried to arrest him, but feared the multitude, for they perceived that he had told the parable against them; so they left him and went away.

¹³ And they sent to him some of the Pharisees and some of the Herodians, to entrap him in his talk. ¹⁴ And they came and said to him, "Teacher, we know that you are true, and care for no man; for you do not regard the position of men, but truly teach the way of God. Is it lawful to pay taxes to Caesar, or not? ¹⁵ Should we pay them, or should we not?"

But knowing their hypocrisy, he said to them, "Why put me to the test? Bring me a coin, and let me look at it." ¹⁶ And they brought one. And he said to them, "Whose likeness and inscription is this?"

They said to him, "Caesar's."

¹⁷ Jesus said to them, "Render to Caesar the things that are Caesar's, and to God the things that are God's." And they were amazed at him.

¹⁸ And Sadducees came to him, who say that there is no resurrection; and they asked him a question, saying,

¹⁹ "Teacher, Moses wrote for us that if a man's brother dies and leaves a wife, but leaves no child, the man must take the wife, and raise up children for his brother. ²⁰ There were seven brothers; the first took a wife, and when he died left no children; ²¹ and the second took her, and died, leaving no children; and the third likewise; ²² and the seven left no children. Last of all the woman also died. ²³ In the resurrection whose wife will she be? For the seven had her as wife."

²⁴ Jesus said to them, "Is not this why you are wrong, that you know neither the scriptures nor the power of God? ²⁵ For when they rise from the dead, they neither marry nor are given in marriage, but are like angels in heaven. ²⁶ And as for the dead being raised, have you not read in the book of Moses, in the passage about the bush, how God said to him, 'I am the God of Abraham, and the God of Isaac, and the God of Jacob'? ²⁷ He is not God of the dead, but of the living; you are quite wrong."

²⁸ And one of the scribes came up and heard them disputing with one another, and seeing that he answered them well, asked him, "Which commandment is the first of all?"

²⁹ Jesus answered, "The first is, 'Hear, O Israel: The Lord our God, the Lord is one; ³⁰ and you shall love the Lord your God with all your heart, and with all your soul, and with all your mind, and with all your strength.' ³¹ The second is this, 'You shall love your neighbor as yourself.' There is no other commandment greater than these."

³² And the scribe said to him, "You are right, Teacher; you have truly said that he is one, and there is no other

but he; 33 and to love him with all the heart, and with all the understanding, and with all the strength, and to love one's neighbor as oneself, is much more than all whole burnt offerings and sacrifices.

34 And when Jesus saw that he answered wisely, he said to him, "You are not far from the kingdom of God." And after that no one dared to ask him any question.

35 And as Jesus taught in the temple, he said, "How can the scribes say that the Christ is the son of David? 36 David himself, inspired by the Holy Spirit, declared,

'The Lord said to my Lord,
  Sit at my right hand,
  till I put thy enemies under thy feet.'
37 David himself calls him Lord; so how is he his son?" And the great throng heard him gladly.

38 And in his teaching he said, "Beware of the scribes, who like to go about in long robes, and to have salutations in the market places 39 and the best seats in the synagogues and the places of honor at feasts, 40 who devour widows' houses and for a pretense make long prayers. They will receive the greater condemnation."

41 And he sat down opposite the treasury, and watched the multitude putting money into the treasury. Many rich people put in large sums. 42 And a poor widow came, and put in two copper coins, which make a penny. 43 And he called his disciples to him, and said to them, "Truly, I say to you, this poor widow has put in more than all those who are contributing to the treasury. 44 For they all contributed out of their abundance; but she out of her poverty has put in everything she had, her whole living."

13 And as he came out of the temple, one of his disciples said to him, "Look, Teacher, what wonderful stones and what wonderful buildings!"

² And Jesus said to him, "Do you see these great buildings? There will not be left here one stone upon another, that will not be thrown down."

The Questioners

THE PEOPLE who heard Jesus each day in the Temple were different from the crowds he had faced by the Sea of Galilee. There were many in Jerusalem who responded to Jesus with enthusiasm, for he continued to tell the wonderful good news of God's love. They rejoiced when Jesus answered the questions put to him by hecklers. But there were also those among the crowds who were eager for any kind of excitement, and there were angry people who were annoyed by what Jesus was saying. They wanted to see Jesus in trouble. Finally, there were Jesus' real enemies, who were doing everything possible to find the means to destroy him. Who were they?

The Pharisees and scribes were his old enemies, and Jerusalem was their stronghold. From the early days in Galilee, certain Pharisees and scribes had been afraid of what Jesus was saying and doing, and they wanted to get rid of him. This was not true of all Pharisees, however, for some of them were friendly. Jairus (5:22) may have been a friendly Pharisee. Nor were all the scribes unfriendly. They believed that the commandment to love was important, and unless one kept this commandment, one's religion did not amount to much.

But it is easy to see why many scribes were suspicious of Jesus. They thought he was not taking the ancient religious laws and customs seriously. These men were sincere in their faith, and they were afraid of Jesus' teaching. Others hated him because they were fakes, and Jesus was against dishonest, fake religion. These men appeared to be very pious. They said long prayers in public and dressed in such a way that everyone knew they were scribes. But Jesus saw through them. Jesus said that if you rented a piece of property from them you should look out, for they would cheat you.

Early in Jesus' ministry, the Pharisees had teamed up with the friends of King Herod to get rid of him. Some of these people were friends or relatives of King Herod, and others worked for him. If Jesus caused a revolution, the Romans would blame Herod, and perhaps take away his crown. So the Herodians, as the followers of King Herod were called, had watched Jesus closely from the very first. And from the very first, they had worked with the Pharisees in seeking ways to destroy him (3:6). Now they tried to catch him with trick questions, such as whether Jews should pay taxes to Caesar. But Jesus answered them without falling into their trap.

The chief priests were new enemies. Only since Jesus came to Jerusalem had they taken an active interest in getting rid of him. Was he not putting his authority above theirs by challenging the way they were running the

Temple? They were members of the Sanhedrin. If they could find a reason for bringing Jesus before that council, they would see to it that he was convicted of something.

Still another group of enemies were the Sadducees, who have not come into the story before. They were members of families related to the high priest; they were the high society of Jerusalem. The principal thing about their religious belief which made them somewhat different from other groups was that they did not believe in resurrection from the dead. They accepted the first five books of the Old Testament as Scripture. None of these books mentioned the resurrection, they claimed. The Pharisees disagreed. Jesus sided with the Pharisees in this, and quoted from the Book of Exodus to prove the Sadducees were mistaken. No one likes to be shown up in public, so the Sadducees became Jesus' enemies.

The Passover

THE climax of the celebration which had brought so many visitors to Jerusalem was the annual Passover meal. You might describe the Passover as being something like a combination Fourth of July and Christmas. It is the Jews' Independence Day, when they celebrate their escape from slavery in Egypt. It is also a religious day, for the escape was an act of God, and the Jews date their history as a people from this great event. It was more important even than Abraham's journey to the Promised Land many centuries earlier. The Feast of the Passover is a patriotic day, a religious day, and a family day. On the Passover evening (you remember that a "day" begins with sunset and lasts until the next sunset), each family gathers together and eats the lamb which has been ceremoniously sacrificed at the great altar in the Temple.

At the supper (Jews speak of it as the "Seder"), the story of the deliverance, from Exodus 12:1–20, is read aloud. On the table are flat hard cakes of bread, called matzoth, into which no yeast has been put. That was the only kind of bread the fugitive slaves from Egypt had been able to eat, since they did not have time to wait for the bread to rise before they baked it. There are also certain bitter herbs on the table to remind them of the bitterness of their bondage in Egypt. Some of the blood from the lamb that has been killed is spread on the doorposts of the house to recall that Moses ordered their ancestors in Egypt to place the blood on the doorposts so that God's destroying angel, who would strike down the first-born of every Egyptian family, would "pass over" the houses and families of the children of Israel. This celebration of the Passover has come down through the years unchanged; it is celebrated in the same way in many Jewish families today.

The Christian custom of saying grace before a meal goes back to Jewish custom. At the supper every Sabbath evening, and at Passover, the head of the family "blesses," thanks God for, his gift of food, and, breaking the bread, hands it to the members of the family and the guests. He also says a thanksgiving over a cup of wine, which is then passed to all.

How wonderful it was to be in Jerusalem to celebrate the Passover! Though many pilgrim families had to camp outside of the city, all tried to obtain a room in Jerusalem for the Passover meal so it could be eaten within the Holy City.

Jesus had planned carefully for this last supper with his disciples. Everything was arranged so that they could meet in a private room. There is a Christian tradition that the house which Jesus chose belonged to the parents of John Mark, who may be the author of our Gospel. Jesus had looked forward to this Passover meal with his disciples. He sat down with them filled with deep thoughts of what was soon to happen.

The Last Supper: *St. Mark 14:1–31*

14 It was now two days before the Passover and the feast of Unleavened Bread. And the chief priests and the scribes were seeking how to arrest him by stealth, and kill him; ² for they said, "Not during the feast, lest there be a tumult of the people."

³ And while he was at Bethany in the house of Simon the leper, as he sat at table, a woman came with an alabaster jar of ointment of pure nard, very costly, and she broke the jar and poured it over his head.

⁴ But there were some who said to themselves indignantly, "Why was the ointment thus wasted? ⁵ For this oint-

ment might have been sold for more than three hundred denarii, and given to the poor." And they reproached her.

⁶ But Jesus said, "Let her alone; why do you trouble her? She has done a beautiful thing to me. ⁷ For you always have the poor with you, and whenever you will, you can do good to them; but you will not always have me. ⁸ She has done what she could; she has anointed my body beforehand for burying. ⁹ And truly, I say to you, wherever the gospel is preached in the whole world, what she has done will be told in memory of her."

¹⁰ Then Judas Iscariot, who was one of the twelve, went to the chief priests in order to betray him to them. ¹¹ And when they heard it they were glad, and promised to give him money. And he sought an opportunity to betray him.

¹² And on the first day of Unleavened Bread, when they sacrificed the passover lamb, his disciples said to him, "Where will you have us go and prepare for you to eat the passover?"

¹³ And he sent two of his disciples, and said to them, "Go into the city, and a man carrying a jar of water will meet you; follow him, ¹⁴ and wherever he enters, say to the householder, 'The Teacher says, Where is my guest room, where I am to eat the passover with my disciples?' ¹⁵ And he will show you a large upper room furnished and ready; there prepare for us." ¹⁶ And the disciples set out and went to the city, and found it as he had told them; and they prepared the passover.

¹⁷ And when it was evening he came with the twelve. ¹⁸ And as they were at table eating, Jesus said, "Truly, I

say to you, one of you will betray me, one who is eating with me."

[19] They began to be sorrowful, and to say to him one after another, "Is it I?"

[20] He said to them, "It is one of the twelve, one who is dipping bread in the same dish with me. [21] For the Son of man goes as it is written of him, but woe to that man by whom the Son of man is betrayed! It would have been better for that man if he had not been born."

[22] And as they were eating, he took bread, and blessed, and broke it, and gave it to them, and said, "Take; this is my body." [23] And he took a cup, and when he had given thanks he gave it to them, and they all drank of it. [24] And he said to them, "This is my blood of the covenant, which is poured out for many. [25] Truly, I say to you, I shall not drink again of the fruit of the vine until that day when I drink it new in the kingdom of God."

[26] And when they had sung a hymn, they went out to the Mount of Olives. [27] And Jesus said to them, "You will all fall away; for it is written, 'I will strike the shepherd, and the sheep will be scattered.' [28] But after I am raised up, I will go before you to Galilee."

[29] Peter said to him, "Even though they all fall away, I will not."

[30] And Jesus said to him, "Truly, I say to you, this very night, before the cock crows twice, you will deny me three times."

[31] But he said vehemently, "If I must die with you, I will not deny you." And they all said the same.

The Covenant in Blood

THROUGHOUT the meal, Jesus was thinking about what was going to happen, and he tried to make this clear to the disciples. The disciples insisted that they would always be loyal to him.

The disciples did not understand, at this time, what new meaning Jesus had put into their last supper together. Only afterward did they see the meaning in the breaking and eating of bread and in the drinking of the wine together. But as Jesus gave them the bread he said, "This is my body," and after they had drunk the wine, he said, "This is my blood of the covenant." And he added that for him this was the last meal until the kingdom came.

The prophet Jeremiah, speaking for God, had said: "Behold, the days are coming, says the LORD, when I will make a new covenant with the house of Israel and the house of Judah, not like the covenant which I made with their fathers when I took them by the hand to bring them out of the land of Egypt, my covenant which they broke. . . . I will put my law within them, and I will write it upon their hearts; and I will be their God, and they shall be my people." (Jeremiah 31:31–33) Now this had come to pass. The eleven (without Judas the traitor) were the new people of God, the new Israel.

According to tradition, a covenant (an agreement or testament or pact) between God and His people had to be sealed with blood. When the covenant between God and the people of Israel had been sealed at the foot of Mount

Sinai, Moses had sprinkled the people with blood. (Exodus 24:7–8) Now Jesus would give himself for them, and for the "new Israel," the Church, his body broken and his blood poured out as the seal and pledge of the covenant. Here, in the simplest form possible, was the origin of the Holy Communion, which was the way the disciples met for worship after the first Pentecost. (Acts 2:42)

Chapter 8

Trials

WHEN the hour of testing comes, it is well to know who are friends and who are enemies. Jesus had many friends in the crowds. There were those who followed him because his presence and words made God seem near and loving and fatherly. There were others who followed out of thankfulness for having been healed, or because they hoped he would heal them. Some, even among the Pharisees and priests, were greatly impressed by his teaching. Then there were the twelve, his closest friends, and a slightly larger group of men and women who were his constant companions.

Yes, Jesus had many friends—but they still did not really understand what he was telling them about his mission, and they were unorganized. They followed him for such different reasons that they were not likely to stand together in his defense.

Nevertheless, up until now Jesus had so many friends that his enemies did not dare to attack him. Now he was in Jerusalem, in the very stronghold of the three powerful groups that hated him: the Pharisees, the chief priests, and the Roman officials. Each group was strong and well-organized and waiting for its chance to put Jesus out of the way.

Until that Thursday, Jesus and the twelve had left the city each evening and gone to the quiet village of Bethany where they were safe. After the supper in the upper room, Jesus changed his schedule.

In the meantime, Judas had gone to the chief priests with a proposition. He offered to lead them to Jesus secretly, if they would pay him. Here was the opportunity Jesus' enemies were looking for, and they were pleased.

As Jesus and his disciples were heading for the Mount of Olives, Judas slipped away in the darkness. The little group crossed the Kidron ravine and entered the garden on the lower slope of the Mount of Olives known as Gethsemane (which means "the oil press," for oil was made here from the olives on the mountain).

Gethsemane, Jesus on Trial
St. Mark 14:32–50

14 And they went to a place which was called Gethsemane; and he said to his disciples, "Sit here, while I pray." 33 And he took with him Peter and James and John, and began to be greatly distressed and troubled. 34 And he said to them, "My soul is very sorrowful, even to death; remain here, and watch." 35 And going a little farther, he fell on the ground and prayed that, if it were possible, the hour might pass from him. 36 And he said, "Abba, Father, all things are possible to thee; remove this cup from me; yet not what I will, but what thou wilt."

37 And he came and found them sleeping, and he said to Peter, "Simon, are you asleep? Could you not watch one hour? 38 Watch and pray that you may not enter into temptation; the spirit indeed is willing, but the flesh is weak." 39 And again he went away and prayed, saying the same words. 40 And again he came and found them sleeping, for their eyes were very heavy; and they did not know what to answer him.

41 And he came the third time, and said to them, "Are you still sleeping and taking your rest? It is enough; the hour has come; the Son of man is betrayed into the hands of sinners. 42 Rise, let us be going; see, my betrayer is at hand."

43 And immediately, while he was still speaking, Judas came, one of the twelve, and with him a crowd with swords and clubs, from the chief priests and scribes and the elders.

⁴⁴ Now the betrayer had given them a sign, saying, "The one I shall kiss is the man; seize him and lead him away safely." ⁴⁵ And when he came, he went up to him at once, and said, "Master!" And he kissed him. ⁴⁶ And they laid hands on him and seized him. ⁴⁷ But one of those who stood by drew his sword, and struck the slave of the high priest and cut off his ear. ⁴⁸ And Jesus said to them, "Have you come out as against a robber, with swords and clubs to capture me? ⁴⁹ Day after day I was with you in the Temple teaching, and you did not seize me. But let the scriptures be fulfilled." ⁵⁰ And they all forsook him, and fled.

The Struggle in the Garden

JESUS was alone in the quiet. It was the middle of the night. That is when a pain is greatest. It is when the imagination paints the clearest picture of awful things which may happen. The friendly crowds were all asleep somewhere. Even in the little circle of his own disciples, Jesus had no one who could understand, and one of the twelve had slipped away. Maybe some of the others would leave him too. The middle of the night is a lonely time.

Taking three of his most trusted friends, he went a short distance from the others. When the going is very hard, it is good to have real friends nearby, even if all they can do is to stay with you. And this is all Jesus asked. "Stay awake. Stay with me. I am going over there to pray. Won't you pray for me, too?" But they soon fell asleep.

Jesus was wide awake as he faced the greatest decision of his life. Was this what God wanted him to do? Or should he escape over the hill before Judas came back? It would be so easy to slip away in the darkness and return to Bethany. What should he do?

At his baptism, and again at the Transfiguration, God's voice had come to him, calling him "my beloved Son." In the garden he prayed to his heavenly Father. Over and over, he prayed: "Abba, Father, all things are possible to thee; remove this cup from me; yet not what I will, but what thou wilt." (Jesus spoke Aramaic. "Abba" is Aramaic for "Father," and so was the actual word Jesus used).

At last, Jesus was sure that God wanted him to face up to his enemies. His struggle with himself in the garden was over. He knew what he had to do. "It it enough," he said. "Rise, let us be going; see, my betrayer is at hand." The temple guards led by Judas arrived in the garden.

Why did Judas betray his master? No one knows. Maybe he had come to believe, with the Pharisees and chief priests, that Jesus was destroying the religion of their fathers. It is more likely Judas believed at the beginning that Jesus was to be a leader of his people in the revolution against Rome, and now he was disillusioned because Jesus was fulfilling the Jewish prophecy of a Messiah who would suffer for the sins of all mankind. No one really knows.

At any rate, Jesus was arrested. And now all of his disciples deserted him, even Peter, James, and John.

The High Priest and Peter on Trial

JESUS was given a hearing before the Jewish authorities. The high priest was seeking to find some charge to bring before Pontius Pilate, the procurator, so that Pilate would find Jesus deserving of death.

The witnesses did not agree with each other, and some of them gave false testimony. It is unlikely that all seventy-one members of the Sanhedrin were present, even if the high priest summoned them, for it was the middle of the night. The high priest had to work fast in order to get Pilate to act before the next sunset, which would be the beginning of the Sabbath. So this hearing was conducted quickly, and in at least fourteen ways it broke the careful rules of the Sanhedrin for a fair trial.

The high priest was trying to find something wrong with Jesus. In a sense the occasion "tried" the high priest himself and found a great deal wrong with him. And someone else was put on trial by the events of that awful night: Peter.

And They All Condemned Him
St. Mark 14:53–72

14 And they led Jesus to the high priest; and all the chief priests and the elders and the scribes were assembled. ⁵⁴ And Peter had followed him at a distance, right into the courtyard of the high priest; and he was sitting with the guards, and warming himself at the fire.

⁵⁵ Now the chief priests and the whole council sought testimony against Jesus to put him to death; but they found none. ⁵⁶ For many bore false witness against him, and their witness did not agree. ⁵⁷ And some stood up and bore false witness against him, saying, ⁵⁸ "We heard him say, 'I will destroy this temple that is made with hands, and in three days I will build another, not made with hands.'" ⁵⁹ Yet not even so did their testimony agree.

⁶⁰ And the high priest stood up in the midst, and asked Jesus, "Have you no answer to make? What is it that these men testify against you?"

⁶¹ But he was silent and made no answer.

Again the high priest asked him, "Are you the Christ, the Son of the Blessed?"

⁶² And Jesus said, "I am; and you will see the Son of man sitting at the right hand of Power, and coming with the clouds of heaven."

⁶³ And the high priest tore his mantle, and said, "Why do we still need witnesses? ⁶⁴ You have heard his blasphemy. What is your decision?"

And they all condemned him as deserving death. ⁶⁵ And some began to spit on him, and to cover his face, and to strike him, saying to him, "Prophesy!" And the guards received him with blows.

⁶⁶ And as Peter was below in the courtyard, one of the aids of the high priest came; ⁶⁷ and seeing Peter warming

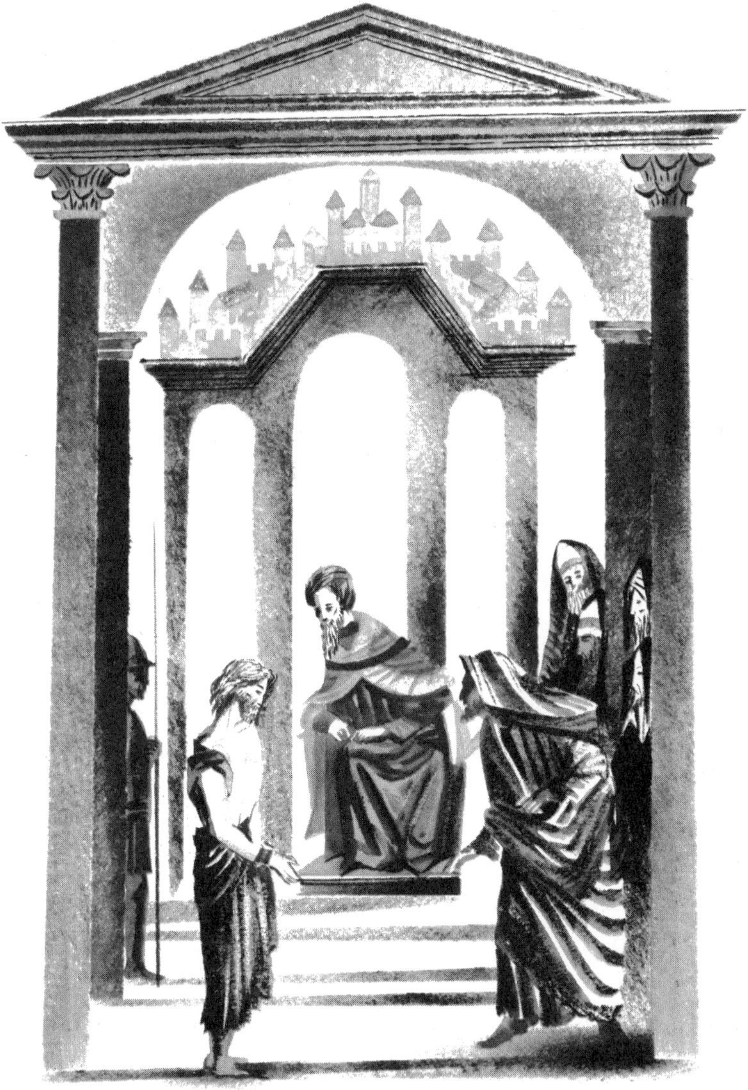

himself, she looked at him, and said, "You also were with the Nazarene, Jesus."

⁶⁸ But he denied it, saying, "I neither know nor understand what you mean." And he went out into the gateway.

⁶⁹ And the maid saw him, and began again to say to the bystanders, "This man is one of them."

⁷⁰ But again he denied it.

And after a little while again the bystanders said to Peter, "Certainly you are one of them; for you are a Galilean."

⁷¹ But he began to invoke a curse on himself and to swear, "I do not know this man of whom you speak."

⁷² And immediately the cock crowed a second time. And Peter remembered how Jesus had said to him, "Before the cock crows twice, you will deny me three times." And he broke down and wept.

Blasphemy or the Truth

JESUS remained silent while all the false charges were made against him. But he answered the direct question of the high priest, "Are you the Christ?" with the words, "I am; and you will see the Son of man sitting at the right hand of Power." For the first time before his enemies, Jesus claimed to be the Messiah. *Power* was a Jewish expression for God. "Sitting at the right hand of Power" was the same as, "at the right hand of God," as we say in our creed.

The high priest claimed that this was blasphemy, which means speaking against God. Now a claim to be the

Messiah was not strictly blasphemy according to Jewish thought, and this charge would not have held in a regular court. But the high priest was determined to have Jesus crucified by Pilate, so he tore his robe (which every pious Jew was supposed to do when he heard anyone blaspheme) and declared Jesus' words blasphemy. All present condemned him as deserving death.

In the early morning, the Sanhedrin held a "consultation." By Jewish law, no actions taken during the night were legal; the council (Sanhedrin) had to wait until after sunrise to act. By this time, the high priest had been able to get together at least twenty-three members, the smallest number necessary for an official meeting. The high priest gave them his report of what had happened during the night: that Jesus had claimed to be the Messiah and had uttered blasphemy. They then drew up a charge to be presented to Pilate, the Roman governor, stating that Jesus, who claimed to be king, was going to lead a revolt against Rome. They said he wanted to be king of the Jewish nation, a warrior, and to lead a revolution against the Romans! Thus Jesus was charged with being just the sort of Messiah which he had done everything to disprove!

Pilate on Trial

WHEN Pilate was aroused, it was still very early. Remember that by nine o'clock in the morning Jesus was on the cross. After sunrise there had to be time for the consultation of the Sanhedrin and the trial before Pilate.

As in the case of the high priest, Pilate, although conducting Jesus' trial, found himself on trial as he faced Jesus.

What Evil Has He Done?
St. Mark 15:1–15

15 And as soon as it was morning the chief priests, with the elders and scribes, and the whole council held a consultation; and they bound Jesus and led him away and delivered him to Pilate. ² And Pilate asked him, "Are you the King of the Jews?"

And he answered him, "You have said so."

³ And the chief priests accused him of many things.

⁴ And Pilate again asked him, "Have you no answer to make? See how many charges they bring against you."

⁵ But Jesus made no further answer, so that Pilate wondered.

⁶ Now at the feast he used to release for them any one prisoner whom they asked. ⁷ And among the rebels in prison, who had committed murder in the insurrection, there was a man called Barabbas. ⁸ And the crowd came up and began to ask Pilate to do as he was wont to do for them. ⁹ And he answered them, "Do you want me to release for you the King of the Jews?" ¹⁰ For he perceived that it was out of envy that the chief priests had delivered him up.

¹¹ But the chief priests stirred up the crowd to have him release for them Barabbas instead.

¹² And Pilate again said to them, "Then what shall I do with the man whom you call the King of the Jews?"

¹³ And they cried out again, "Crucify him."

¹⁴ And Pilate said to them, "Why, what evil has he done?"

But they shouted all the more, "Crucify him." ¹⁵ So Pilate, wishing to satisfy the crowd, released for them Barabbas; and having scourged Jesus, he delivered him to be crucified.

A Roman Court of Justice

WHEN Pilate had heard the claims, he asked Jesus if he would admit the charge. "Are you the King of the Jews?" Jesus replied in stern dignity and with disgust, "You have said so" (which might better be translated, "Those are your words, not mine").

St. John's Gospel tells us that after questioning Jesus, Pilate "sought to release him." (St. John 19:12) Look more closely at the reasons why this did not happen.

We know what kind of people the high priest and the chief priests were. But who composed the crowd which they so easily controlled? Every other crowd that had gathered around Jesus had been friendly. Only this one was unfriendly. Why? Who were these people? Were they the same pilgrims who had waved palm branches and shouted in his honor five days earlier as Jesus rode into the city? Perhaps some of them were. Were they people who had listened to Jesus as he taught in the Temple? Those listeners had been so friendly that the religious authorities had been afraid to arrest him in public.

It is more probable that this crowd was made up of Temple guards and others who worked for the high priest. Perhaps some of them were slaves. Some could have been men whom Jesus had driven from the Temple for selling animals and changing money in the Court of the Gentiles. Others were idle bystanders who gathered because of the early morning excitement. No doubt Barabbas was popular with some of them. Many of the pilgrims would not yet have come to this part of the city, it was so early.

At any rate, the people who gathered at Pilate's palace were willing to let the high priest tell them what to say. "What he wants is good enough for us. If he likes Barabbas better than Jesus, so do we."

And where was Roman justice? Even if the high priest was determined to destroy Jesus, shouldn't the Roman governor have been just? Pilate was no fool; he could see that Jesus was, as we would say, being framed. He knew Jesus was being mistreated, that he was not a dangerous revolutionary or guilty of any real crime. But Pilate was weak; he thought more of keeping his job than he did of doing right. He wanted peace at any price. The Romans were afraid of crowds, for crowds are hard to control once they get started. An angry crowd could start a revolt against Rome, and it was Pilate's job to keep revolutions from getting started.

Then Pilate outsmarted himself. He offered to free

either Barabbas, who was a prisoner and obviously guilty of murder during an uprising, or Jesus. He probably thought they would ask him to free Jesus, but they asked him to free the murderer and to crucify Jesus.

So in his weakness, Pilate sentenced an innocent man to death. The high priests had won. Or had they?

Chapter 9

The Way of the Cross

ST. MARK tells the story of Jesus' suffering and death with remarkable restraint. He provides us with the facts, but he does not enlarge on them. A scourge is a whip of cords or thongs, sometimes knotted or tipped with metal, attached to a handle. Jesus, as a man condemned to death, had no rights; the soldiers could do with him what they pleased.

After the terrible scourging, St. Mark describes three other scenes: the mocking by the soldiers, the march to the place of the execution, and the hours on the cross. The first took place in Pilate's palace, the castle of Antonia which overlooked the Temple's outer wall from the north.

Here the whole Roman battalion of about six hundred men gathered to make fun of the one who, they had been told, claimed to be the king of the Jews. They indulged in some brutal horseplay, and the purple cloak and crown of thorns were used to show what they thought of this king. They were showing their contempt for the whole nation by making cruel fun of this "king."

The second scene was on the street that has come to be called the Via Dolorosa, the Street of Sorrows. Crucifixion was the Roman way of putting unruly slaves to death, as publicly and as painfully as possible. They made the victim carry the heavy crossbeam. The upright post of the cross was left standing in the ground from one crucifixion to the next. Jesus had received especially cruel treatment and was exhausted from his beatings, so the soldiers compelled Simon of Cyrene (a city of North Africa where there was a large Jewish colony) to carry Jesus' cross. That a stranger was drafted to carry the crossbeam indicates that the pictures are correct which show Jesus falling from exhaustion.

The crucifixion is described so completely we can almost see it—the suffering, the unconcern of the soldiers, the cruel laughter of Jesus' enemies who have finally destroyed him, Jesus' words from the cross, the death and its effect on the Roman centurion. Here is an event to ponder. What does it really mean? Throughout those long hours Jesus remained clearheaded; he refused the offer of drugged wine which would have dulled the pain.

And Was Crucified: *St. Mark 15:16–39*

15 And the soldiers led him away inside the palace (that is, the praetorium); and they called together the whole battalion. ¹⁷ And they clothed him in a purple cloak, and plaiting a crown of thorns they put it on him. ¹⁸ And they began to salute him, "Hail, King of the Jews!" ¹⁹ And they struck his head with a reed, and spat upon him, and they knelt down in homage to him. ²⁰ And when they had mocked him, they stripped him of the purple cloak, and put his own clothes on him. And they led him out to crucify him.

²¹ And they compelled a passer-by, Simon of Cyrene, who was coming in from the country, the father of Alexander and Rufus, to carry his cross. ²² And they brought him to the place called Golgotha (which means the place of a skull). ²³ And they offered him wine mingled with myrrh; but he did not take it. ²⁴ And they crucified him, and divided his garments among them, casting lots for them, to decide what each should take. ²⁵ And it was the third hour, when they crucified him. ²⁶ And the inscription of the charge against him read, "The King of the Jews." ²⁷ And with him they crucified two robbers, one on his right and one on his left.

²⁹ And those who passed by derided him, wagging their head, and saying, "Aha! You who would destroy the temple and build it in three days, ³⁰ save yourself, and come down from the cross!" ³¹ So also the chief priests mocked him to one another with the scribes, saying, "He saved others; he

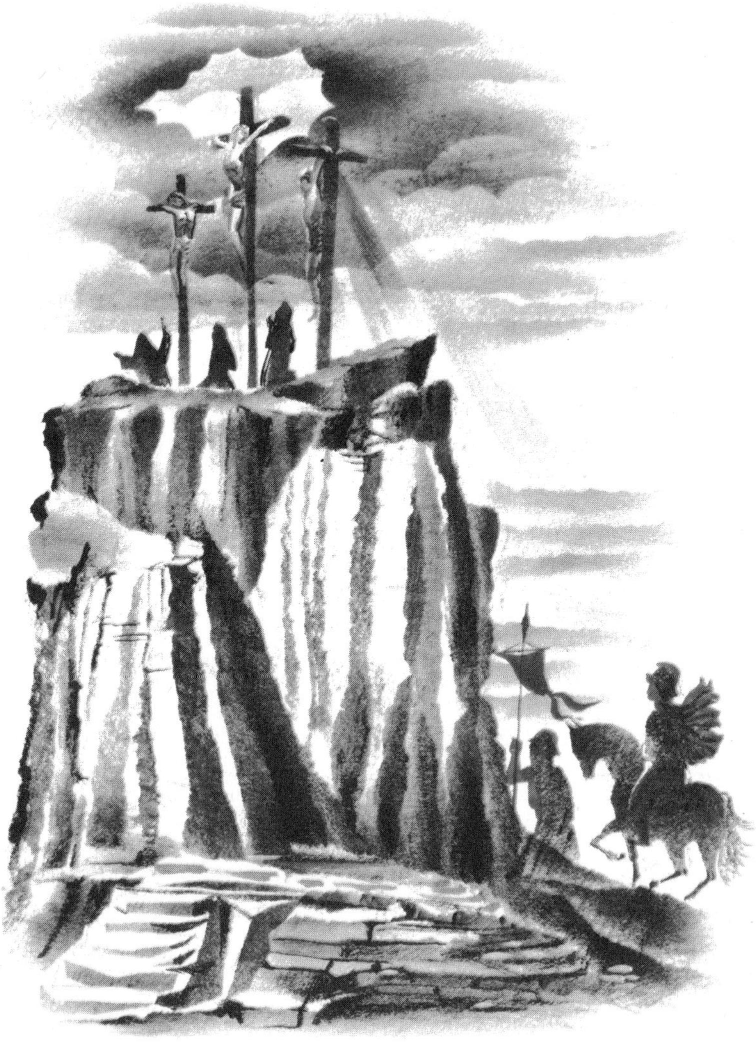

cannot save himself. ³² Let the Christ, the King of Israel, come down now from the cross, that we may see and believe." Those who were crucified with him also reviled him.

³³ And when the sixth hour had come, there was darkness over the whole land until the ninth hour. ³⁴ And at the ninth hour Jesus cried with a loud voice, "Eloi, Eloi, lama sabachthani?" which means, "My God, my God, why hast thou forsaken me?"

³⁵ And some of the bystanders hearing it said, "Behold, he is calling Elijah." ³⁶ And one ran and, filling a sponge full of vinegar, put it on a reed and gave it to him to drink, saying, "Wait, let us see whether Elijah will come to take him down."

³⁷ And Jesus uttered a loud cry, and breathed his last. ³⁸ And the curtain of the temple was torn in two, from top to bottom.

³⁹ And when the centurion, who stood facing him, saw that he thus breathed his last, he said, "Truly this man was a son of God!"

The Great Shout

As Jesus died, he uttered a great shout of victory. Even the words, "My God, why hast thou forsaken me?" were the beginning of the twenty-second psalm, and the psalm ends with hope:

THE GREAT SHOUT · 115

> "Men shall tell of the Lord to the
> coming generation,
> and proclaim his deliverance to a
> people yet unborn...."

His was not a cry of despair or of relief because the pain was about to end. It was a shout of victory. Battle accounts tell of the shouts of the victors. Jesus died a victor, a shouting, triumphant hero. The Roman officer was amazed. This victim of Roman cruelty was no ordinary man, "Truly this man was a son of God."

Chapter 10

The First Easter

THE DAY of the crucifixion was Friday. It has become for us "Good Friday." The Sabbath began at sunset, and the crucified body had to be buried by that hour. In order not to break the law of the Sabbath, the body had to be in the tomb before sundown. It took courage for Joseph of Arimathea, a member of the Sanhedrin, to ask for the body. In so doing, he was publicly criticizing members of the Jerusalem council who had brought about Jesus' death.

The tomb was cut straight into the side of a hill. The rock on both sides of the Kidron ravine was quite soft. A great stone was rolled against the opening of the tomb to prevent dogs or jackals from getting in.

There had not been time before the Sabbath began on Friday at sunset for the women to buy the spices and other things they needed to anoint the body. The Sabbath ended at sundown on Saturday evening, and then the shops were open again. The faithful women bought the spices and planned to go to the tomb early the next morning. This, they thought, was the last thing they could do for Jesus.

But in the tomb, to which they had come in sadness, they received news that filled them with wonder and astonishment. There *was* something more important they could do for him!

The Glorious Surprise
St. Mark 15:42–47; 16:1–8

15 And when evening had come, since it was the day of Preparation, that is, the day before the sabbath, ⁴³ Joseph of Arimathea, a respected member of the council, who was also himself looking for the kingdom of God, took courage and went to Pilate, and asked for the body of Jesus. ⁴⁴ And Pilate wondered if he were already dead; and summoning the centurion, he asked him whether he was already dead. ⁴⁵ And when he learned from the centurion that he was dead, he granted the body to Joseph. ⁴⁶ And he bought a linen shroud, and taking him down, wrapped him in the linen shroud, and laid him in a tomb which had been hewn out of the rock; and he rolled a stone against the door of the tomb. ⁴⁷ Mary Magdalene and Mary the mother of Joses saw where he was laid.

16 And when the sabbath was past, Mary Magdalene, Mary the mother of James, and Salome bought spices, so that they might go and anoint him. ² And very early on the first day of the week they went to the tomb when the sun had risen. ³ And they were saying to one another, "Who will roll away the stone for us from the door of the tomb?" ⁴ And looking up, they saw that the stone was rolled back; for it was very large. ⁵ And entering the tomb, they saw a young man sitting on the right side, dressed in a white robe; and they were amazed.

⁶ And he said to them, "Do not be amazed; you seek Jesus of Nazareth, who was crucified. He has risen, he is not here; see the place where they laid him. ⁷ But go, tell his disciples and Peter that he is going before you to Galilee; there you will see him, as he told you."

⁸ And they went out and fled from the tomb; for trembling and astonishment had come upon them; and they said nothing to any one, for they were afraid.

The Mystery

THIS is the way St. Mark's Gospel ends. That it stops so abruptly, on a note of silence and fear, has bothered many scholars and been the cause of much study and many theories. Some scholars think the Gospel was longer and that the original ending was lost.

The "lost ending" theory is based on the belief that St. Mark would not end his story with the words "they were

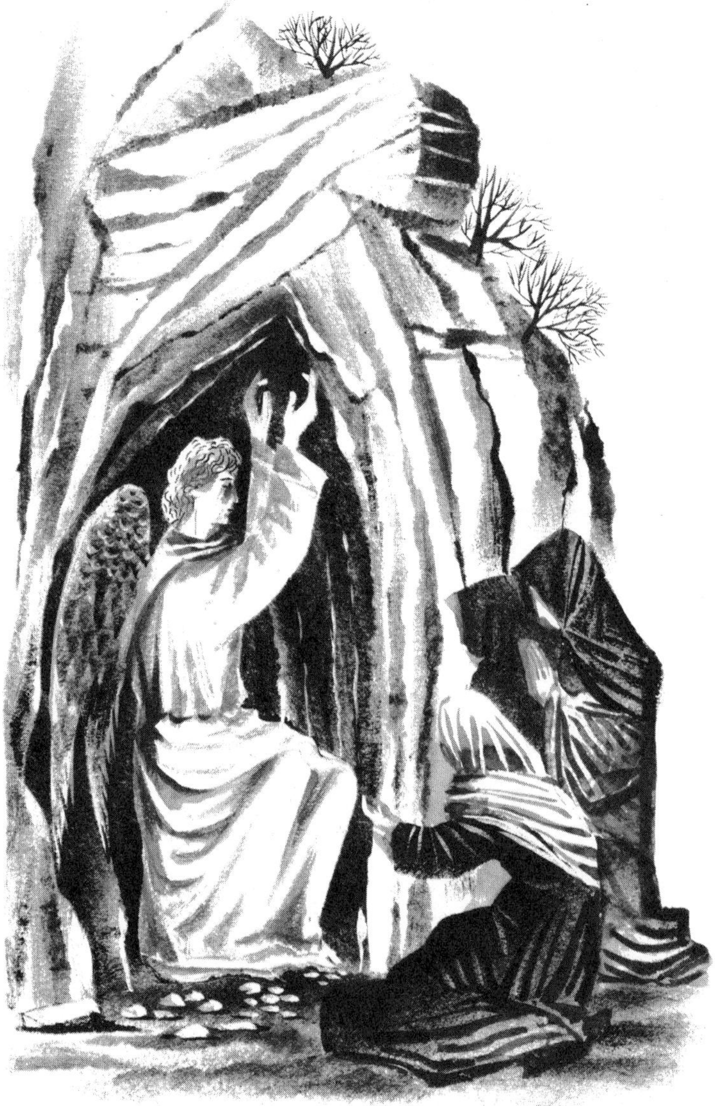

afraid." This seems all wrong after what he has written about Jesus, picturing the power of God as working strongly through all that Jesus said and did.

It has been suggested that the original ending of the Gospel was torn off, perhaps by an escaping Christian who was trying to save the scroll. According to this belief, the Gospel we have today is what he was able to save. What he left behind was the final column of the manuscript. If some non-Christian had found just that one portion, he would not have understood what it was all about. Jesus would have been a mystery to such a man. The "lost ending" would have been thrown away.

Since the second century, Christians have vainly tried to supply St. Mark's "lost ending." One of these attempts is preserved in our King James translation of the Bible (16:9–20) and is also found in a footnote at the end of St. Mark's Gospel in the Revised Standard Version. Because St. Matthew and St. Luke used St. Mark's Gospel when they wrote their own accounts of Jesus' life, copying much of it, some scholars think we can find the original ending in their accounts. A few think it is in the added ending to St. John's Gospel (John 21). No one has the answer, and the "lost ending" theory remains a puzzle for all of us.

Another way of looking at the problem is that there was no "lost ending": St. Mark finished his Gospel just as we have it, with verse 8. What more do we need? The angel tells the whole story in three lines:

"He has risen.
He is not here.
See the place where they laid him."

Of course the women were astonished at this news, but we know it is what happened. No other details are necessary. St. Mark ends his Gospel with the great fact of every Easter: "He is risen." The Gospel is never finished. Christ lives still, and we need to add our own ending, our record of what Jesus Christ has said and done through us.

St. Mark's Gospel is the story of Jesus Christ, the Son of God, as the opening sentence states. Jesus became conscious of his mission or task at his baptism (1:11). No one else knew, except the demons, and Jesus kept the demons from telling his secret (3:11–12 and 5:6–13). Finally, Peter realized who Jesus was and announced the news in front of the disciples (8:27–30), but Jesus would not let them tell the secret either. Also, it immediately became clear that even Peter did not really understand Christ's mission (9:31–33). Three times Jesus explained that he must suffer and die and rise again before he had completed his mission (9:9–13; 9:30–32; 10:32–34). The disciples still did not understand, perhaps because they wanted Jesus to be a different kind of Messiah (6:52).

As soon as he had risen from the dead, however, the disciples did understand. Then, when they looked back over what Jesus had said and done, the followers realized what he had been telling them. St. Mark is saying that Jesus

Christ is a mystery, and no one can understand him until he believes in the Resurrection. The important thing is not how Jesus appeared to the disciples after the Resurrection, but that he should be present to each of us, and speak to us as directly as to his followers in Galilee and Jerusalem during those months that changed the history of the world.